RED STRAWBERRY LEAF

PHOENIX POETS

Red Strawberry Leaf

Selected Poems, 1994-2001

JOHN PECK

THE UNIVERSITY OF CHICAGO PRESS
Chicago and London

JOHN PECK is a freelance writer and editor, a practicing analyst, and the author of seven books of poems. A fellow of the American Academy in Rome since 1979, he is also the winner of the first annual Thomas McGrath Prize in poetry.

The University of Chicago Press, Chicago 60637
The University of Chicago Press, Ltd., London
© 2005 by The University of Chicago
All rights reserved. Published 2005
Printed in the United States of America
14 13 12 11 10 09 08 07 06 05   1 2 3 4 5

ISBN: 0–226–65294–7 (cloth)
ISBN: 0–226–65295–5 (paper)

Library of Congress Cataloging-in-Publication Data

Peck, John, 1941–
  Red strawberry leaf : poems, 1994-2001 / John Peck.
    p. cm. — (Phoenix poets)
  Includes bibliographical references.
  ISBN 0-226-65294-7 (cloth : alk. paper)
  ISBN 0-226-65295-5 (pbk. : alk. paper)
  I. Title. II. Series.
  PS3566 .E247R43 2005
  811'.54—dc22

                                        2004016394

Once more to the memory of
Johannes Felbermeyer,
gentlest master

I will penetrate all the depths of the earth, and look on all who sleep, and enlighten all who hope in the Lord.

S O P H I A in Ecclesiasticus 24:45

Far off I saw a great black cloud craning over the world, drawing earth into itself and submerging my soul, for the seas had penetrated even to her, polluted by the deeps of hell and shadowing death. For a storm over-came me. Black creatures grovel and lick my earth. Therefore my flesh sickens and every bone twists. . . . He who digs for me and brings me up as treasure, who does not trouble my tears nor mock my foul dress, will leave my meat and drink unsullied, my bed undefiled, my slight body unviolated and above all anima mea, a spotless dove full comely, nor will he mar my seats and thrones: I languish for his love, in whose heat I melt and in whose odor I thrive, whose sweetness heals me, whose milk feeds and whose embrace makes me young, whose breath inspirits me, whose kiss quickens and in whose clasp my body trails lost—him shall I father as he fathers me!

Both artifex and Sophia, in parable one of
Aurora Consurgens, attributed to the dying T H O M A S   A Q U I N A S

When rays from the awakening one streamed into me, my body reached past all the worlds, and my belly grew as vast as space though it stayed belly. The marvelous marks of the womb that rests everywhere, the home of all awakened ones that spreads through the ten directions, all these appeared in my body.

Q U E E N   M A Y A   D E V I ,
mother of Prince Shakyamuni, in the Flower Ornament Sutra

Contents

Acknowledgments · *xi*

I

July · *3*
Barn Doorway in July · *5*
Inhaling the Pequot Dynasties · *7*
The Bench at Fontainebleau · *9*
Medley of the Cut · *12*
A Twenty-fourth Poem about Horses · *16*
Thucydides · *21*

II

The Granite Steps at Sunrise · *27*
Three Tongues · *29*
Pines and Hemlocks · *35*
Heaven after Moving House · *37*
Anangkē · *39*
Letter to Hermann Broch, December 2001 · *42*
A Metal Denser than, and Liquid · *56*
Barges at Koblenz, 1986 · *61*
At the Atom Plant near Vernon, Vermont · *63*
Transmission Lines · *65*
Single Wing · *74*

III

Conus Marmoreus, Night Piece, Rembrandt · 79
San Andrean One · 82
San Andrean Two · 93

IV

Carnival, Luzern, 1984 · 107
Inkbrush Strophe and Antistrophe for Juditha, 2000 · 109
Porter of the Oar · 111
Max Beckmann · 114
Little Ode on Wheat · 117
Eclogue · 119
Little Testimony at Fruitlands, Massachusetts · 121
Rhyming with Davie's Sonnet in Mandelshtam's Hope for the Best · 125
A Stock-Taking :
   Inventoriable · 126
   Walter Benjamin's Hope for the Best · 127
Unfinished Announcement · 130
Adventus · 133
Passage · 135

Notes · 137

Acknowledgments

Grateful acknowledgment goes to the editors of the following magazines in which these poems first appeared:

Agni: "A Twenty-fourth Poem about Horses," "A Metal Denser than, and Liquid"
Boston Review: "Barn Doorway in July"
Literary Imagination: "Pines and Hemlocks"
Notre Dame Review: "The Bench at Fontainebleau"
Orion: "Eclogue"
PNReview: "Letter to Hermann Broch, December 2001," "Little Testimony at Fruitlands, Massachusetts," "Transmission Lines"
Salmagundi: "Adventus," "Little Ode on Wheat," "Max Beckmann"
Samizdat: "Medley of the Cut"

"Single Wing" and "Walter Benjamin's Hope for the Best" first appeared in *Inizia* (Rhino Editions, Magnolia, 2001).

Thanks also to the Author's Guild, Edward and Sheridan Bartlett, Ellen Peck Killoh, and David Oswald for support. And to Professor Thomas Cassirer and Dr. James R. Scherer for valuable information.

I

July

The chapel with frescoes along one sun-warmed wall
gave onto a railway cut, its footpath
pushing afternoon into a far province,
a low jet fighter repealing its wrath like rolled tin—
I was forty-three and investigating my blindness,
advancing into what it had darkened me to see,
and so the pale devil herding mannequins
and the swirlers even paler over them, counter-herding,
had moved slightly as I moved, they were the left hand
which Kant says in mirrors turns into the right hand
yet is neither, a third thing, its raised scar transposed—

if I had stopped then,
if I had let the roar roll me back
which until then had been packed, trembling, inside,

I would have missed around the turn
three scythe-men in file up the slope of the cut, each with one leg
crooked at ease, at pause in their green swaying notches swabbing sweat
then raising their hats in slow arcs, no halloos—
for the gesturing hand does not catch what is falling
but holds wide the opening that is rising,
even after a shout staying wide for stillness—
and so they rose there, the age of angels
when air, having come to maturity, allows breath that has
circumnavigated the globe to slouch down

and take on body, say, fifty and a bit overweight,
faded suspenders up through the bagged-out shirts—

and I waved back, and turned, and felt
the bolt unslip its catch on a paint-swollen door
that leaned out once into a summer that now was.

Barn Doorway in July

Where may heart open through the lockstep of evil and good?
Weathered doors divide along a rail on dot wheels.
Blurred, the hankering for harvests. No one stands there,
while midway a shaggy sphere of petals, and bees stirring
geranium eternity, weave scent and low sound.
Faint essence that quilts the commander-in-chief's guilt
as he treads the red weave to his bath, sealord sacrificer,
and quilts too Lulu's shriek, cradling wrath and frail form
while the hum thrusts melody from her first seed—
this hangs by chain, flows from a tub of garden pinks
dealt through chalky whites: commonest companions
hosting hummingbird now and a star's heat, those
interlacing frequencies wrap-thronged and arrowed.
Contemplation is the wing, sang the Victorine.
Here it whirrs to feed on light, its other self.
Ever from two, all the rest. From that, a portal.
And then darkness, musty generations of grass ghosts,
swayed spines of milk's bearers twitching off flies.
Captain, courtesan, those stained excellences,

$\qquad\qquad\qquad\qquad\qquad$ go through.
Why have all other eyes watched them if not for this.
When I thought I had missed destiny, these
gathered and passed, startling pair though inevitable.
No bridge from death in the bad to death in the good, declareth
the whole, ant's mandible nibbling what the shark dribbled,
yet that couple strode over into forgiveness and vanished.

When it is too much, and when it is never enough, the doors
have been, already, drawn open over this cooling cave.
Across the unblazed trail with the trodden, the threadbare with the fresh.
And if that is so long since, I must have witnessed it.
Though blank here, I am in the knowledge. And souls, the bees.

Inhaling the Pequot Dynasties

Emerging into a judgment
while the judge avoids decision—
moving toward distillation
while the day backtracks to complexity—
pushing out through varnishes
in the celebrated Van Eyck Wedding of the Arnolfini,
pushing to breathe—

past a bellied mirror gathering back tucks in a gown
that greenly poses a baby's bulge:

wanting, having, and being married to that—
civic religion since the caves—

as a swimmer towards the blue roof he would shatter,
so with everything in my body
pushing to pass these, to come out.

Ribs a strongbox near bursting, yet the eye hooks
into convexities, stray brightness, vignette
of the body's Holland swallowing inshore
negotiable chubbed hulls that rub their strakes
and thwarts against each other,

all this indeed presses in: did I use it that long ago, and now
again do they hoist it with cable through wet creakings?

Dutchness unharbors goods from a mummy chamber's dollhouse,
buddingly as the grape's hazed cluster-clutter,
shadowing each comparison, measuring, knicking the notch.
The other making, the imperishable, breathes everywhere but is not seen.
Maya means measure. A wind ruffles roadsteads
gray-green from the unmeasured, out of the unbounded
tilting ever so slightly the painted hulls—

then it cores open,
when I break surface and bob,
parachutist with the soft staggers,
grass whispering by my waking eye, fresh damp and esters,
the familiar and the strange in one usage.

In the middle of a city block, oak-stained silence
of the dinosaur hall at age eight—
whoever is here now a moment ago was not.

Continually many wake towards being one inside a surf
rolling the globe, and thus it happens, a drawn-out
trumpet voluntary, behind the eyes Spring.

The Bench at Fontainebleau

forty years after the Nadia Boulanger workshops

Out through the gate, yet not
out of its shadow, ruddy
stone over passages
to those cool hedges on raked
pathways, it hangs through years—
iatros, the invasive
word of surgical harm,
knife of delving and red
damages, is it your
harsh therapy I wish
to visit on the place?
In one way, yes, I was trying
to emerge from heavy flesh:
towers of the first
François, the embracing spill
of stairs where Bonaparte
abdicated and where
the Austrian corporal climbed
to taste triumph. But then
a lacey matter, gauzes
floating from practice rooms
in the inner court, filmily
erased the rest, drifting
across formal gardens
to constitute the new
medicine itself, even

if broken, studious,
and reaching for effect
in ten directions and
with twelve means—the summer
conservatory, its fabric
forming in the air
with every torsion of
the weave, anticipating
the wrapping of every kind
of wound. So. Yet sound
was not there. I'd sat through
some earlier drift of it
out of those windows. That
was alright, quite alright.
And now that the knife seems a false
solution to the lengthy
illness, infection
spreading not from a palace
but the fountains of blood in the mind
no one shuts off, the surge
from below, fluid thrust
taking one always from
below—now that such cutting
relieves
        nothing, it is
the nothing that yields to flowing
phantasm and hard practice
that soothes, and not only soothes
but jets strength. *Have you heard it?*
asks the spiritus rector,
and I say *No* while shaking
my head *Yes*. And I ask
you, my listener, myself

down the future: *Have you,*
too, heard it? The gardener
props an ancient bicycle
against the privet, and spits.
That is in real time. And in
the other time, its jumbled
measure flowing from
those high caves, I will then
say the contradictory
same. Already that thrust
throngs here articulating
pattern that moves through
and around, weavings of
a practice known from before
but half-forgotten, known now as
capable of dissolving
architecture because
it is the architect:
it is the fountain though
I do not name the water,
one does not name it, that water.

Medley of the Cut

The column of the commander yielded to our first sweep.
Even the water jar for our diggers we set on the south wall
of the general's tomb without knowing it. So we began.
His armies retook Nubia, Libya, and the Levant,
lost under the sway-bellied lantern-jawed Sun King.
Overseer of all scribes, Overseer of the priests of Horus,
Grain-giver to all lands, Royal chief of staff, Regent,
the general had himself carried on his palanquin
through the wailing processions
to oversee the work on this place. And so carved, thus:
one of his men punches a Nubian in the face.
The general was low-born; everything had counted
and he knew what counted most.
His platoons lift open palms towards Tutankhamun.
The general towers as a sway-girdled go-between at court
for beseeching Libyans.
Only the pearl-handled revolvers do not figure here,
or the comeback challenge *Nuts!* in the Ardennes winter forest.
He had himself carried beyond the busy streets of the dead
in the city of the dead sloping back from the bluff
to a higher, private terrace looking across to Memphis.
But then he rose to Pharaoh. So he is not here. Instead
his first wife lay here, and then his queen also.
At his own royal tomb in the Valley, where the designs
remained uncarved, sketching idea along stone,
he does not rest either. The fine picklock hand

got past Anubis and the reared serpents, and got to him,
the Lord of Upper and Lower Egypt. It got past Truth
with her high feather, which moved at the slightest disturbance.
The general did deep obeisance to her. He is not here.

What at last moves the heart?

So much already moved, even in his own century,
architects prying loose mud bricks of the core for new tombs.
Cult funded in perpetuity gone in two generations.
So Coleridge, who was indisposed that day, prudently
remained in the circle of lime trees while his friends went off
on their walk through the countryside. He followed them in his mind.
That way no one would have to dismantle Horemheb's outer court
to secure bricks for the statuary room, and facing stones.
He cast his mind outward, a net over his dear ones,
sending them at pace through the middle distance of steeples,
hill lines, and the murder of Lamb's mother by his sister,
a brief madness, thus through the appropriately middle distance
where such things are built and performed in fact, no closer, no farther,
then on out to the cleansing rim of apocalypse, evening
in the bath of waning fire, one bird stitching
the whole veil of showings tight along its upper hem—
though he was not there, he could tell them that none the less
he was next to his words and his word was with them, even
unto the rim of their wandering and their turning back.
One dome of air and fire. But he was not there. Nor I here.

What removes the heart from what moves it?

As if I were the lecturer before a congress of doctors,
his clinching point approaching, when suddenly he stared out
in silence, and at last said, *Ladies and gentlemen, esteemed colleagues,*

the only thing I can see at this moment inside my brain,
such as it is, is a little white mouse chasing a little white ball.
Their laughter recovered him. But he'd found he was not there.
And Nietzsche smooched the dray horse. Soon, too, he was not there.
Or rather in five places, seeking cartage, and thinking he'd found it.

What removal does not pass through the rippling pump room?

The G.I. whose father had been raised in a Swiss house along
one of the lakes knocked, in uniform, and asked to see it,
and conned the dark-paneled ceilings, and drank Schnapps, and took
photos of the owners. And then he knew he was not there.

Where is the room if it always surrounds you?

An interviewer came to Thomas Mann after the war, from Italy.
The interviewer was a poet. Mann offered him no coffee, and
called him *Signor Mountainous*. Not there, the poet.

The *Riss* between body and soul, the ancient killing fields
of Prudentius, Pauline salt poured in the cut, that rift
deeper than the Mariana Trench: these are the gift of all
dualisms, a yawn between detaching spacecraft shooting
over the blue-white swirl between continents. *Nicht da*,
that separation widening to meters, we see the not-there.

What moves but the heart?

If you wait for the sun to take it at the slant angle,
and if you gaze at his crouched form long enough, then
it will move. At ease on the general's head and fish-like hands
floats the *djed* column, its foliate
abundance, leafed powers, stemming out to the solar bud.

He rises beneath it and there is no strain on his face,
valves of space intervene between the stone and his palms,
its basal flare like a parasol shelters him, who under
any other circumstances, in that spot, would be red gristle.
Twelve tons, but chiseled at the requisite depth he goes in
beneath it and rises. Light with him. And he's not there.

Nor are you there, finisher still here and breathing me, though
steadily you intimate such. But paradox is your *forte*.
You whose touch lifted this very weight for awhile
pass, fluttering interpreter
of the last things in our tawdry updrafts of the fake,
the last first butterfly. My brothers maintain
that the hot wind is friend, lifter of stones, trembler of heavy
horizons, for they half-remember that for them you vanished
into ripples at the join of sky and dust, until
the column floats only because they are no longer
aware that they stagger beneath it. And I with them though
I am not here, having been grazed by your wing, its razory mercy.

A Twenty-fourth Poem about Horses

Night deepening, frost leans on the stables
of thoroughbreds, west wind splitting their hooves.
—LI HO, "Twenty-three Poems about Horses"

Steed out of my dusk and a dusk, now, for the species,
veins deltawise down your silky inner thigh,

veins trickling from one eye down the roan cliffside
of a nose vaulted and chanceled for winds of the Pleistocene,

you have come, you paw patiently, that is the main thing,
the fields between stretch wider and we, the restless, are everywhere

save where your nostril quivers, arches, and you snort in the night.
We who debouch into all places dream of you now nowhere.

You come to a woman's hand: that smile. You come to a
child's hand, giggling and shivers. Your hot breath pleasures soldiers.

Harnessed to caisson with bannered coffin, to the barouche
at a state wedding, you are ambassador from the eldest kingdom.

The King of Brazil sent a forest of teak to pave the streets
girdling the Pantheon, to muffle the clatter you hauled there.

When we spurred you against Wellington's infantry squares,
you side-ran them or reared back. The god of catastrophes took note.

Sad banner you were in the prophecies of Sweet Medicine,
the whiskered whiteys bringing and spawning your manes and tails

among the Arapaho, Cheyenne, Lakota, Kiowa,
your speed between their loins a drumming into decline.

Under Tutankhamun, the generalissimo who rode you hummed
his tenth title: Overseer of Works in the Hill of Gritstone,

while there in those Works among the pulling men pulled also
your brother, sent down because of a freakish temperament.

Muir knew you on both shores, and van der Post knew you,
mufti lords recognizing a lord in service. Nuzzle them both.

They say that Poseidon at Onchestos, breaking you as a colt,
had your driver leap off where the road entered forest,

and watched to see what you'd do, the rig rattling—smash it
against the trunks on the run, or walk it through tall shadows.

Where you linger for shade on the veldt, branches level,
a tree is the only tree. Your water, the only water.

Flickers of hair along your neck's crest release
the only signal. Which staggers from storm cloud to browse oats.

Stubby melted candle, your recessed phallus makes
no howitzer but glistens a coat whose sheen ripples off.

For I imagine that Li Ho, seeing good men misused
as you were, foresaw your withdrawal from our night grasses.

For your standing here re-ordains neither Akhilleus
nor Cuchulain. Dew braids your mane with fresh constellations.

For what shall we make of you, made into goddess, mare
sacrificed but receiving cult also among the footloose

on the steppes: mother ridden by god-spear, great mam thus
captured, cinched, spurred? though your flanks shudder unfettered.

Through mists we flash bits of mirror, but from them
you pound abreast, neither parent, eyes orbing the two sides.

For that demigod's eye, tiding, capsizes anyone
who would turn trainer. And this goes on into the bond.

A trainer aims at one thing, but what tingles him is force
hinting at the uncontainable, the opponent.

And the top tamers, spook-soothers, the whisperers,
will write their books but miss the appointment. It is not inscribed.

The two grooms beside you in Hokusai's whitewater cascade
lave you with splashes of it, currying your bulk,

hoisting your nosebag—and no one has set the timer, everywhere
it is one sound, stampede steadied and rocking in it.

Your great-grandparents, unicorn wild asses
from Persia and Scythia, fostered childbirth but also pissed plagues,

the unharnessable *summum totium* browsing in ocean,
an eye-spangled three-legged mountain. Hell and cloud in your seed!

It was your miniature stature at the beginning, Maria Tallchief
at ten, that wedged you between giants into the straightaway.

And the reindeer modeled from smudge in the Font de Gaume grotto
at Les Eyzies, fading across your body, trails a third antler

like a skater's scarf through your head, broadening out,
a dancer's arm rippling after the total gather.

Looking back from the pass at his mounted escorts, flashing them
three turns back down the corkscrew, the Fourteenth Dalai Lama

saw them slumped on your back, the red of Rahu in splashes
and trickling stillness. And dripping you still awaited their nudges.

In that patience, the kernel of the twister moan-lifting
over Kansas, the shrapnel clatter of your take-off.

Across that aftermath, bubbling through wind-sound or the mind's
rise from its cringe, the flubber-flutter of moody-moodlessness.

So the unforeseen from you opposes the blindly seen in us—
your fuse as a spurter, jump-taker, yet a curb also

to our unsnaffled berserkness. For the berserking Greek says
that only that ass's horn or hoof, cut off and cupped upward,

can hold any of the cold torrent under the world,
implacable Styx. All else, graces or muons, it crumbles.

And every jot which that flow dissolves, the images
with their assessors, has rolled in us. And you have stood

calmly beside us, your shot breath a bloom in the cold,
your hooves hammers yet also the last and only chalice.

The unreached-for cup, beaker for world-toxin,
breast englobing ground zero. And so we know you not.

And I realize: though I have walked drenched in spring rains
my bare thighs have not hugged your warm bellows in a downpour.

For though your manic tribe is mine, the boreal chargers,
mere rooms, a migrant's mangy stations, have detained me.

For while historians of cultures hot on the spoor of roots among
their root clans have heard you drum past, they looked up only briefly.

For though engravers assumed you would stay, given their way with your
musculature, accoutrements, wavy harness, tip-toe grooms,

gear draped over your cruppers like an evening gown, its ratios
and metalwork continuous with Genghis Khan's and a jockey's,

their inky mastery frames cosily misleading questions:
which posthouse this evening, what pasture tomorrow?

Whereas you inquire into rupture and the unfenced: what thunder
between flesh and ground, what surge from the cells even past sundown?

Thucydides

The pachyderm smooth-trunked straight-limbed
beech is an admiral—
trireme-sweeps down each leaf,
flotilla arrays of foliage
prow to prow at anchorage—

and all wear the gold of the dead
through December, shrugging
the pollen of our plagues
with January's powders.
Return of the fleet! Corridors
through masts, and yet I'll dare
to pray with my keel and prow,
offering my hold half-empty,
aiming them through years
at the unnamable dear source.

The historian skips this: renewing
the offering with what one is.
The entire Greek saga
is a badge we pin on our shirts
to pretend that we have the smarts
of berry hunters in Paraguay
or New Guinea. We do not,
though favored by place and the powers!

With renewed passion to share out
my bilge gravel to spirit.

The fat man from Thrace,
MacArthur's arrogance
(to list the rest would be
my arrogance), *Fortune*'s
republic at anchor with urchins
starve-gazed in the glossy
annual reports and Yuletide
gift campaigns—these the ships
will last out and push past as
the Persian dead at Salamis?

Each hull's footprint with the oars
overlayed in one green
telegram, one trim stanza
cutting more seas than a raft
of prose—and so will that gift
bring immunity? fleets
hanging flat through the seasons as
vast inoculations.
   Haudenausee, canny
Haudenausee, Seneca

wiped from your villages
by Washington with blankets
as the bait, pox-laden,
you spoke of another matter,
the quite ponderable matter
of lost balance, growth
to delusional reach, and a great
purification, which even

Greek fire loosed from those ships
cannot hold back. Perhaps

it will not come. But you
indicated the sign:
first no berry, and next
a red strawberry leaf
in its place. That, enough

to release the big speech
from all the traduced powers,
from everywhere in them at once
thunder or quiet to roll on
and on, no historian

scripting it for a mere mouth.
Nor is that likelihood
my ground, nor the wide water
between your emptying
and mine, nor my boat, nor any thing.

II

The Granite Steps at Sunrise

Day Lily stalks have lowered their flags now, turning
ivory with tobacco, bones of stork saints pitchforking morning.

Last night cold in the headlights, a motorist
dragged a dead doe from the shocked lane, his steaming wreck plumed with
incense.

It is a medium city nestled in hills.
The terminator of darkness has just slid off its rim like a flashlight's,

the river through its mill-strewn aorta declares
water's completion of this shelter from wind and malignant disturbance.

Now over Songwang-sa, the first licks of cold
from high Siberia are held off at the north by sentinel mountains,

and in the meditation halls they're completing
their long day over ondol floors with fire channels just lit this season,

while postulants stoking fuming vats of rice
pour in leftovers crouching near their flap-capped columnar stovepipes.

So it was warmer underfoot than this is,
when Master Kusan brought his years of push to an end while standing

through one full week. Somewhere over the rooftops
the high-pitched belly whine of sirens homes on need at its sharpest.

When I was as high as those stalks, I stood looking out
over front steps to a road at evening, the steel district tucked under,

everything seamless one moment inside and out,
sensing the vast world balanced and thinking: *This could all be quite different.*

Every fire at simmer in out-of-sight foundries,
and in the rooms behind me, and behind my eyes, entire. And it could be.

Three Tongues

The more it gets released
into itself, the first
plane of our nature, the more
its ceaseless breath drives off
the already-thinning veil
of cloud across hills
and fields, and the harvesters
lean through. Whitman has gone
from the wards home to his memos.
The smell of the contests within flesh
follows and vertigo
steeps in, yet that compaction
clarifies him: *affection*
first, and other medicines
afterward. . . . He has told me
since that this little visit,
at that hour, just saved him. . . .
On his skin the tang
of oranges from the boxes
he handed out in hot weather,
an expansion from steady compression,
trodden and fenceless, the air
of Virginia *a rich and elastic*
quality by night and by day,
vastness standing forth
into great space.

                    Rising
into the mirror a face
exchanges left with right
and emerges, not quite across
and not between yet partaking
of a dense co-inherence
clarified. *I think sometimes*
to be a woman is greater
than to be a man—is more
eligible to greatness,
not the ostensible
article, but the real one.
And the warm oranges, and
a heap of amputated
limbs outside the window
into the field, have siphoned
into that tight smooth warp
between the two faces and pressed
back out again;
                    so where,
and who, and has not the calm
come with you regardless?
                              Full
of breadth, and spread on the most
generous scale, and the noise
of the axes sounding sharp.

        *   *   *

Between the plucking and the being-eaten,
quiet days in a cool crock on the big table.

Fruit: there is no estimating it. Best to kiss it.
Before devouring it one is still there, in the chink called existence,

and can circulate within its hungers, tower along them
as the hawk off a thermal's shoulder, not yet scanning, perhaps free

in the bowl of wind. Rounded, rounding, and, upswing
into the last turn, heaved weightless yet body-full.

Plotinus's eyesight was so poor that he could not read
the Christian tracts. But what he plucked from his tree

gleams in the bowl on the table in the room
I know I shall find again. Though nearsighted I saw it.

The Pittsburgh I saw as a child at night
became a legend of flares and slag pours—

the furnaces came down, but what they released
on the retina still rotates and glows

as warrant for the bowl, plum against fuzzed peach,
drawn-out harvest, ripenings within ruins,

and so it was for questions he fielded from his gaggle
of Romans, respecting their grabby minds

as his own guidelines while an unending
sentence responded through him, from the orchard's

hundred trees but to one round sweet point,
where there is no room for florid talk,

or time for ambling to the edge of the sunned meadow,
or drifting to the cataract's lip

out into fullness, for the whole thrust is there and one is
in it, turned because no more room comes in which to turn,

it is the room and that lariat sentence floats, and you are what
you have been waiting for, the sentence spreads your table

oiled and polished, the layered clay
of the brown bowl and in it mounded

cousinships of death soaking seeds,
all of it there, the point. And his wide hands.

*   *   *

I clambered down the raised beach to wet sand, no bathers
in mid-August, the drench and drain lifting sight outward.
In wavered a speck steady on its heading, butterfly lifting
over my shoulder and showing itself cloak-black
with burnt orange trailing edges,
not the species named for grief, with blue droplets
and yellow rim, but another emissary sans portfolio.
It made for my things up the sand, hovered over them,
then lighted on the raised stones behind, wings panting,
palpating tons of rubble.
                    All brave effort bears tone,
yet trembling out like shimmer from sheet metal, person
shaken down into person then shot out, the non-similar:
he spoke yet I could not hear him.
    His fuselage was manufactured in a webbed hangar,
soft rivets, slow conga-line of landing gear, blunt bomber nose,

then junked unfinished, mummied snug, left for plunder,
swallowed. For he took our century's body into his body
for digestion, in him the thing went down. Ate his youthful shell
then ensilked himself to be eaten. Famishment for alteration,
jaws for himself, then mouthless: instarate, chrysalate
in leaf litter, he is what he'd awaited
yet his wings are not coupled, he cannot chew, sipping
salt ichor from sand, and the varied honeys, a straw his sole means.
And then he must search for her. And so, surf-skimmer, was I
your Marilyn, my unrolled bath-towel your boudoir? Unerring aim,
though the heart-spark in you has footed, then slumbered, then flown,
morph to morph. Each time your force transits it spills nothing,
and though one being pops out each time, a throng rides it.
If the tone goes, it is like a chorus sliding offstage in the opera,
their cry finished and hanging, with only the swish of their skirts.
You must understand, said the many, *we are few.*
Our elders led us here in promise yet it turned bad.
Our dead before the walls we cannot claim and bury.
Repeatedly the high geese snare our wails and vanish.
Incognito a young king strapped on bird-catcher's wicker
and whistled forth the young queen in scullery skirts.
The smile which they hide arches a wing's hint, the pressures
linking their hands are a deer's against nibbled saplings
past every wracked thing they have done in the press of fatedness.
Exeunt.

      Whereas you transit past blood, your float shivers
singly, remedy thwacked in the palm of the homeopath,
and shaves into the clearing
where the shift claiming place in us pushes and we look up.
And so I listen for your inaudible directive.
No mandible for chawing, no throat to croon the Blues.
You pump and sail.
        The body

within your body has given away teeth and larynx
to lever air in the great movement, at ease
though it pump and sail and hunt, mate, sunbathe
on the given stones.
                    May all who emerge
be thus safe from themselves, incalculably at wing
in the vast rest.

Pines and Hemlocks

In Longfellow's corridor, a plaster Zeus
bulks as hugely as the Greek replicas
through Goethe's Roman rooms. And a wall plaque
floats one head on a Roman swag, hair noosed,
neck scarfed—like Danton but thinner, aberrant,
Petrarca and Cochise in a fused profile
to authorize a path yet unplotted through vastness
still opening then, before the War, before

the second nation. No identity
pegged for those high cheekbones, yet he blesses
such thrust. Nameless, yet he squired seed and granted
particular dominion over a vague
prospect populous with hope. The murmuring
stands, unsurveyed, communicant with his lips
at rest, brush their progenitor then sleep.
And who will have kindled and baked there, by streams

gone to lead in the gloaming, what they speared
by day: are they his sons also? The smell
of a fresh catch is not that bad smell which
the Yankee lights around a Brattle Street table
brought dripping to book, and bagged. Clean stench, fresh-gaffed
and filleted, blesses and fathers the other work
of sepsis, bone web springing white through flake rot.
And I also stand son, and father. . . . Father:

all rumor of his passing has passed from me
months at a time; no praise from his friends and workmates
reaches me on the living air, they being
gone also now. The simmering of pines
at evening, soft footfalls on a hot pavement,
alike concentrate into the sounds they are
simply from the autonomous mask of struck
and sliding surfaces, unfathered, free.

But sweetness at times—not as in the life,
where it flowed shut—but sweetness, then, the surge
will rise at no interpretable turn,
as when I rounded a stone tower en route
to a train by the river Aare, wet snow in patches,
floodlights etching the rustication. Thus
comes his available spirit. No face, but flow
completed yet still reaching. The wild comes

thus homing, sweetness in a standing wave,
high on a shore unforeseen, and this meeting
establishes the republic: divers lean
and slice the sinuous muscle of swelled current,
leaving the gnat-flecked air to wait, then surface
pouring, catches in hand, and from their eyes
the homes, the rooflines shine, and it is not yet
more than right abundance, nor need it be more.

Heaven after Moving House

Cloud, they say, *Nebel, nuage*; *sunset*, they say—
quintessence of one cycle and yet what do I see?

Anvil. Lozenge. Tongue . . . but I catch myself:

poets in my country have made programs—
either Orwell's transparent pane of glass,
or curves for the sake of curves, disdainful lace
and a high chuckle flaunted into the dark,
or refusals to be co-opted, avoidances
of using language as used by the greedier users.

Well: some of my tables I've made. Others I've bought.
And what has sheltered me I have not built

nor could have. I leave it with some rupture
but no pang. And what I find on leaving,
if I see straight, is roominess. The cleared.

None of our claustral programs lives there. Dante,
Vallejo, left such spaces, and entered them.

Take down the house, even, and angles stay which
they savored, the rains through them, far cloud, suns.
Vallejo, Dante: blowtorch-stares through our programs!

Have I not yet made my pact with them? But I'm moving
some last things, and glimpse my vaporous icon:

anvil: lozenge: bodiless tongue—lavender
through it, flocked pink as the day rolls off—

my finished cycle deals it, yet what am I seeing?

Lozenges melt on the tongue, and on an anvil
either of those . . . or is it their terse triune,
an oiled press ready to go smash—
its forming plunger about to splay the pliant
prong or to pulverize a remedy?

I see what I made of one day yet cannot untangle it,
and seeing that, at least, is honorable.

The pact, if it will be made, will be. Entangled
I spoke, I did not speak, I gave succor,
I forged and flailed.
                              And I did what I could
if truly I chose the best for my limits and powers,

we too sucking medicine from the flame,
we too shaping the flange, sweated lips parted,

and the world stands there, and it hangs there deep
in that light. And we are busy there, and at rest.

Anangkē

Called? I am called to assess all of my relations
before leaving, in loyalty to them. And to see
    from necessity, not only with the light of sensing.
Necessity the fierce at last hangs cleanly lovely—
    it *comes to be,* not pretending to be convincing—

so even if I want to work out patterns, control them,
trail the dovetailing interlocks with my stubby fingers,
    that is not in the cards, *anangkē* has something else
less straightforward, more brutal, in store for me,
    raising a shaking house while setting me inside the walls.

Anangkē can do without its legion of visionaries—
it resumes in each plain pot or fragment. Necessity
    humors but does not require Alfred Watkins on horseback
envisioning from a Welsh hilltop a net of ley lines
    webbing the whole of Britain, glowing against black.

Necessity toys with but does not depend on the web
of dates that Azariah de Rossi strung from King
    Nebuchadnezzar, working out missing chronologies,
cribbing clues from Erasmus and running the calculations
    where no rabbi had sniffed, through all the genealogies—

thus the net, bright space, thick time. Necessity
indulged Azariah, making him its computer, yet

renews itself in unloved sciatica, in garbage at curbside
after the collectors have vacated, in fish hawk
   rapacity training itself to plunge at harborside.

And my own habit, since the first years, of sensing
a pattern of meaning through the lives of high-strung similars,
   as if steering by their winking returning beacons,
has only seemed to be necessary. Though as immediate
   as the taste of ice cream, behind it hangs dawn wisp and wakens.

Anangkē is the unanswerable communiqué
from *le vrai dieu* by whatever name to the worlds,
   leaving them netted breathless, imposing silence on them.
Yet *anangkē* has a shyly persistent sister, the Tao
   by whatever name, whose breath crosses all the way to them.

My fascination with Watkins and de Rossi
bobs on that as a flotsam, no index to such power.
   Even aging, the sentimental lockstep of my clock,
may not point to it. *Anangkē* spoke first to me
   when I was six, on a family pilgrimage to New York,

led by mother up the tower of Riverside Church,
the sexton by mistake having let us scale
   openwork stairs into the belfry near noon.
The ringing began. I clung to those iron stanchions until
   a coaxing cop pried me clear, leading me down.

Revisiting my seed form, there near the tall lancets
that sweep in the Hudson, Grant's Tomb, the seminary,
   and a Harlem that was Merton's, Simone Weil's, Bonhoeffer's,
I see now that none of that fated bricolage
   or those spirits—one of them preeminent among lovers

of necessity—is meant to hover over my little boy
and inform him, through me, of the point. For he had got it,
    and now he relays it again: to hang there—in the power
that he felt as fear and which I might decode as wonder—
    is to float wide of all these through after-strike and tremor.

Not the crude visages of Grant's generals in the crypt,
for their carver has caricatured necessity—
    and not wrinkling water lights under the Palisades
as a migraine halo of necessity for those three
    warrior souls. Perceptions are forever asides.

Azariah saw straight through the Talmudic legends
of Titus's death from a brain-eating gnat, but *anangkē* eats everything—
    Japan's dust still airborne, my kid breathed what the Cheyenne
and Lakota and Hopi, our Tibetans, had seen of our end
    with more than the light of the eyes. Not anything less, then—

only my call to stay there within the grip of the greater,
not above things, really, but entirely within them,
    only their iron and bronze command: you do not know
when nor can you say how, but altering swiftly,
    and opening entirely, it is, and it will go

fully on, becoming what it will be—if war
then so, if interregnum then again so,
    in its intersection seemingly nowhere near ground
with air and light altogether in free
    movement. And you have been the thing struck into sound.

Letter to Hermann Broch, December 2001

So the new unit ticks over. The persistent, faintly detectable taste of time—
    but shall the wine taste itself?

  Twenty-five years back I rented the rooms you inhabited
      at the start of your USA *transitus*.
Third-floor New Jersey rooms grace of Lili Kahler, their walls
    pitched inward with the roof.
Your tenancy there evoked only a faint presence, but now
    words to you become possible—
the vulgarity of this fictitious intimacy meant to be overheard
    will have to do, but you got over
your superstitious regard for the seminarians of literature here
    so let us converse anyway:
Horace, vintner bookkeeper, though not in your Teesdorf textile
    factory, shall watch over us.
A family business, ranks of steel spinners, watched over you
    as you fed them substance and thrived
as one of those who make things go in order to go at things
    with the comb of aristocratic
dragging, the *Schriftsteller*'s calling, on all fronts: not
    the emperor's man but Maecenas's
nephew needled by seeing—not once forgetting the women
    of Buchan pouring sheep piss
on raw wool down their long tables and chanting, whaulking it
    in their rocking stoop, brushing hair back

or wiping a nose: not once dropping a stitch between
    that swiped finger in the keening
and a lady's crooked finger at the *Staatsoper* lifting
    from lorgnette and woven shawl.
You wanted for a Europe climbing down into the pit
    the simultaneous mind,
a long weave and tight thrust of the weft down all strands
    whap at the same force and holding.
I know my countrymen: if they read this they'll pretend
    to be students *But I don't know his books!*
and so, laughing, I write it to you and throw it at them,
    I too wanting the tight weft
across the full loom, and no excuses, and no
    shame about picking noses.
An older friend from Berlin, collecting your poems after
    your death here, sorting through them
and counting, was suddenly moved to improvise doggerel:
    Er bohrt sich handlos in der Nase,
versetzt damit sich in Extase!—and that homage
    was no adolescent wordplay
but a Berliner-tipped hat to your Viennese spark, and the childhood
    of the language he shared with you drumming
beyond your verses, the light in them shooting up. It was the finger
    both of you gave the *Führer*,
and the dactyl that saved you by drumming the right noise
    as you beat your retreat, and
the finger of fate, which you followed by spelunking forward,
    your ears as long as the Buddha's.
And may be a bodhisattva's in fact: you gave yourself.

    Twenty-five. And when you got to those rooms with your Virgil-book
        it had been three or more

since your *Nachtwiese im September*: the illuminated furriness of an
                                        English garden—
    your lines had predicted it,
passage beyond home and its prisons in stripped clarity,
        alien plantings as waystation
en route from spinners and jail to swells of North Atlantic:
        meadow lapping its own edges,
night silver spreading grassy veilings while you queried your spirit,
        the power biding those edges:

> *Can you, mortal thing, by patrolling*
> *the meadowy bounds of all that stays hidden,*
> *can you still make your way back,*
> *perceiver and never knower*
> *to those estates where laughter*
> *and the intoned phrase make their home?*

    Gray walls, and evasive presence: not quite there for me then.
        Ready to host you, I found
your might and span among angular snuggings and stuffed chairs.
        Among them you had Virgil
kill off his poem (or so he thought: Augustus pulled it away
        in his little red wagon
for the ages). *Perceiver, not knower*: the vintage stops there.
        For shall the wine taste itself?
Guilt and the guiltless, sleep among the properly sleepless—
        they still debate these your themes
in Germany, to their credit. Austria is another matter.
        Yet there were reasons for
your scripting Virgil's folklore wanhope over his poem's trek through
        transits and refoundations.
For giving him bad nights, when even Franz Stangl once head of Treblinka
        shortly before he died

told Gitta Sereny he woke from deepest ease, profoundly refreshed.
        Were one now to speak of what art is
George Oppen would be there, another man born to wealth
        and rattled by conscience (I borrow
his phrase *what art is* from a poem on labor) and so
        would use what a worker sees,
but would also mark that worker's evasiveness. Whose *Kitsch* takes vows
        to return only as itself
in a crèche of itself, as brassy *Madonna* goes to Rome
        to have her baby and step out
behind opaque shades bearing swaddling into the flashbulbs.
        And one would have to speak
of elites as if they were another mass, of sleep
        stung into half-alertness,
innocence rattled but still intact in its perception
        of itself. One would, that is, I would
exercise the bad manners of thinking aloud in verse.
        As you forced prose towards philosophy.

    Were I to speak of art now I'd have to listen past
        wakening oppositions—
past inaugurals that flare up in exasperated dismissal
        then settle for bitterness:
an educated woman in Cairo blurting, *If I had one bom-ba*
        I would throw it at both of them,
your president and bin Laden, they are both simplifying demons,
        there is nothing to choose between them—
one would have to listen past governments, false storefronts,
        oppositions as seductions,
past names of opposites of fronts of governments of the peoples
        into how the writer shuts down
and lies down as did your Virgil submitting to *something else*
        that comes up with shoots in the humus

of the field, not drumming but pushing past itself
     to sentinel the night meadows—
no retreat here from *ethics* into *nature* but rather
     a flexible sentry posting,
at verges where the blades springily silver and bend and
     scythe over and rebound.

   Yet such oppositions whisk me off into an easy,
     therefore false totality.
So were I to speak of art now I'd also have to say how
     your effort, dear Senior, thrust towards
total remaking though *handlos*, surrendering past the destroyers
     to something else's hands.
Of *Exstase* only from that, burrowing where the victors
     had beat things flat in order
themselves to stand as totality. I'd have to speak
     of justice—and of the revolving
equilibrium called peace I should have to perceive
     justly, seeing it as the young
Ascanius of justice, his father reminding that child: justice
     favors none, choosing all.
Is the tone, but no single phrase.
                         Yet that might be enough
     to have Virgil lay aside
his poem, perceiving the totality that you shot for
     through him, the span cracking, and
lodge in fevered sleep in Brundisium. Or Connecticut.
     For the tone, were one to speak of it, hums
the fate of impercipience much as our long-eared ones
     follow solar winds belching
from coronas to snuff out every light in Quebec
     and mold baby stars to teardrops;
hums the fate of profligacy much as the clouds

of battery acid on Venus
swirl intestinally over the ooze of silicate volcanoes;
    looms out the web of timespace
as one fabric, in which the chief debtor nation
    no longer appoints the world-bookies
to cook the books in its favor but is made to pay the price.
    Were one to speak of art now.

  But shall the loom weave itself? The eye engrosses what it sees,
    itself it sees not, until evening,
a padlock clamping the store's corrugated gate-screen,
    reveals to sight's blood-soaked velvet
in its wet cave the hoard on all those dark shelves.
    Perceiver and not knower,
for it is enough to see how much there is to perceive.
    Were any to speak of art now
the implications of seeing such would remind them, me with them:
    culture does not make morality—
it busies itself believing that it does, all the while
    inducing heightened morale.
Esprit. Intensity. Bonding. Clarified kinship libido.
    But not necessarily the good.
It kindles the fire circle's gabble, the laughter ring that makes
    grassy the singing phrase.
Philipp Fehl, also from your Vienna and not yet art historian,
    interrogating old Nazis
before the Nuremberg trials in his crisp U.S. Army uniform,
    was quizzing Hans Frank, also
born in Vienna, Hitler's Governor General of Holland.
    Older Philipp leaned towards me
to mimic his fellow countryman leaning towards him:
    "But tell me," he interrupted

in the tones of a gossip or a relative, "Is the opera house
     still standing in Vienna?"

   Black uniforms under the gold galleries: Don Giovanni
     sinks through red puffs of dry ice
on the spook-orders of a virtuous general in stone—
     crash of applause, they are all dead,
but to their descendants hang hungry in the air, raising
     bickerings among the chroniclers:
whom art touched, gilding their faces in rows, do they stir the pot now?
     Who wanted to touch art.
Who made off with trainloads of it. Johannes Felbermeyer
     who worked for the Americans in Rome
as photographer, and was raised by the Munich elite, painting there—
     Vee ver zee first "grass-people"!—
Johannes who knew Lady Hanfstängl who clucked over Hitler
     at her soirées, crouched for three years
over his lens at The Collecting Point in Munich after the war
     recording recovered loot,
Nah-ja, zee writing-desk off Napolyown it vass yust so,
     and thirty off zose Roman heads
I haff explained you, viss drill marks in zee hair?
     Zecond zensury, zee best.
And Fulbright sent MacLeish with questions about all the movables,
     thus came The Collecting Point,
and the inventories, and the assignment of returned goods
     sometimes to vanished houses
or houses with new owners.
                              Helmut Strobel who surrendered
     by waving a white silk scarf
while landing his fighter on a Yank runway—*And the man*
     who ran up to me there
could have shot me but instead handed me a cigarette,

and you Americans have been my patients
ever since—young Strobel lay on a darkened troop train beyond
      Dresden when they bombed it,
his home town. So on his consulting room table lay
      a gnarled bubble of ceramic,
the one bit he'd pulled from the ground. Eighteenth century, the best.
      It didn't help his patients
but maybe the fire would do that. As your folklore Virgil
      supposed it would help his poem.

  But then if it *had* burned, no Aeneas would hover
      over Europe, and the North Atlantic
Turbine, and Bleeding Kansas, and the Golden Gate, and then
      over Siegen, not far from Aachen—
no epic descent to unfurl a drop-screen behind George Stout.
      He scanned the 109 pins
on the Third Army's maps, all hidey-holes for art,
      and picked Siegen—Charlemagne's relics—
and went while there was still shooting, and found the mine,
      and found the town jammed in there,
smelly and frightened and hating the *Amerikaner*,
      a quarter-mile of faces,
and a boy took his hand, smiling, and walked with him,
      and finally the vaulted room
with moldy racks of paintings and the manuscript of
      Beethoven's Pastoral Symphony
and the relics. When he left, not the ghost of his father
      or Tiresias but none the less
a crazed old man followed screaming things about crimes.
      If fire had consumed the poem
we wouldn't have heard Stout speaking beyond himself,
      from the grass past the cave. . . . So, you both saved it.

The Chinese box of conscience! a Roman tomb at its heart,
    for Viennese Aeneas.
Totality of effect and wholeness of obligation
    in one syntax were your aim—
young Ascanius already imperial yet leading
    the funeral games for his
Trojan grandfather on cleared Italian ground,
    stepping his horse through Troia-maze.
Your own son was safe. But your felt duty, your sense
    of the undone, given your privilege,
ate at you as if you had abandoned a child,
    driving you, doing you in—
and so the adoring women could not ease the strangling
    drag of that tiny corpse?
May it be long since of comfort to your shade
    that here, where he slowly killed you
in the way your bridge-building Roman and Viennese honor
    fittingly allowed it,
that our heritage is mixed past resolving: Vietnamese children
    adopted as Rome's own,
and the same children also as warm-up practice for GIs
    pitching C-rations at their heads.
One redeems the other? Of course, yet in our drama
    they remain *all at once*—
one of the ways you taught me to read the living text.

    Not for children, such reading.
And none of the Polish, Ukrainian, or even German children
    from fourteen to under six
from the DP camps, slave laborers, came to my own town,
    a haven for Slavic refugees.
The orders to ship Russian children—to Australia, Canada, the USA—
    were fought by relief workers

who already had uprooted them a second time
    for return to their parents. No records
in Washington remain. From the Ukraine and Poland, stolen
    to the Reich, then pried loose again . . .
and there, my Senior, the attempt of duties to improve on rights,
    your theme, out-Solomons Solomon.
Simply perceiving that tangle clearly is enough—
    of *knowing* it there is nothing.
Love of children: in this country something of a cause,
    fantasied as a pure good—
but then Iraq for a decade, embargoes that choke off medicines
    and dig thousands of tiny graves.
The demon of comparison would steal the facts (we claim we no longer
    steal or enslave children)
but the demon of high innocence looks past them, even
    damning the soundness of those
who lift the veil and point. A seamless veil, but not total.

      Returning to this country
from years away, I found for more than a year that my sensing
    stayed constantly alert
to the chance of inchoate and ubiquitous violence;
    that a familiar chauvinism
and boyish *bonhomie* both served its uncannily hovering
    blood path to guiltlessness.
What I sense does not drag me into the Cairo woman's
    dismissal, or my own
distaste for *Madonna*, or what the Japanese during the War
    pictured as one of their own
pure females brushing her hair free of our *extravagance,*
    materialism, money worship—
it is more intestinal. And perhaps encompassing.
    Had you known our marines

sent scoured skulls, *the little apes,* to their sweethearts?
　　We too have had our race wars.
While Ascanius stays in the poem, and you brought only your case
　　of bad conscience, the boy
has been cut loose here without parent and without horse,
　　on the lookout for funeral games
unaware that they ignite and prance in his past.
　　The haze he moves through, you see,
holds my own shadowy anger as well as your shelter over
　　an exhausted conqueror
of epic spaces and their opaque openness,
　　insomniac at Brundisium.
Not one anti-Ascanius, but two: in the forest gangs
　　of postwar Germany
among once-captive children, and then, through your simultaneous
　　syntax, my nephews here.
The child you did not incinerate wanders here fatherless, free,
　　polluted and purified.
You're absolved: you had nothing to do with this, and the bridgehead
　　of the unburned poem arcs past it.

　And so, by way of codicil, valediction, and parting query
　　let me reweave your own theme:
too beautiful, *too* much, is totality of effect—
　　harmony in the chord
standing on thousands of feet? concord in the surface
　　sprung from the striven-for pattern?—
this false analogy gleams none the less with a menace
　　lived out by defaults
to fault, by cave-ins to a crowd-cave resonant
　　with unauthored authority,
its cushioning, beckoning, mothering, and yet cold-void
　　thrill: *You need not decide.*

A fight means special conditions. The fight is for rights. There are
   unfortunate consequences.
Of course you wanted nothing more to do with make-
      believe. And you did give it up—
but only to the mass-grip of the power drive that lobbed you
      into orbit. The one sacrifice
that cleansed your instrument: *Take it Kaesar it is yours.*
      Yes, grant me your way to those
last grasses, limber through payment of the whole fee.
      But not your drivenness.

   And let me give you a reader's report, things being the same
      yet different. And report on readers—
you felt awkward at Yale for lacking degrees, while they had them?
      but a finger shows the way,
it digs beyond vulgarity or rhymes rooted in childhood,
      in the meadows of blessed *rien*.
Père Henri Le Saux, from India weighing the commentators
      who intone the ancient Rishis,
found them flawless on their elevated plane, yet always
      lacking a certain something—
or rather *a nothing*, indefinable, which none the less
      opens onto the great sea
and even spurts out of it. Father Le Saux in his bare feet
      comforts me in my freelance
business flounderings, bare-bummed in the decades of USA opulence
      and client-state management.
No logic there, my Senior! Nor do I attach myself
      to your Spartan income here
thereby exalting my ineptitude. Yet I smell the *rien*
      in its silvery uncombed meadow.
Inept, too, like you before the best of those readers,
      I am ready to kneel down in worship . . .

when a bit of the wild man sticks my finger up my nose.
    For the professionals in my day
have taken the part of Francesca in hell. They side with the Dante
    who faints with pity at her story,
she having excused herself by testifying to the book's power
    over her, a well-juiced romance.
They throb with the Dante who faints with pity, whereas Dante
    portrayed himself as an object
of impressionable inadequacy and moral weakness.
    He did this to teach readers not
to trust their swooning moods and persuaded affinities.
    Firmly, yet with kindness.
Yet the paid readers intone the phrases with hollow laughter,
    scuttling the bite in the phrase.
They point at the teaching within or beyond a sounded phrase
    to render it skeptic—they make
the intonation in order to laugh apart from it.
    Teacher! He taught us in vain,
argue the professional readers in my own generation,
    because his own art seduces!
We are no longer sitting talking in a Viennese coffee house,
    we are paying for lectures in Athens.
Yet my narrative sophists do not push diagnosis far enough.
    Yes, Dante sweetens his medicine—
but the justice for which he speaks above the sloshes of pity
    is stronger *beyond* his page,
in the sunlight through his rooms in Bologna, Lucca, Padova,
    and terminal Ravenna,
as in the moonlight on and beyond your page in England.

    Your bridgeheads, and the *paradiso*
babblings, aim *beyond*, at that which works *here*.
    A light quiet though from

solar fusion furnaces, a brightness which, once
     I shut my eyes to it,
reddens faintly while filtering through the lids' blood,
     a second shining, its child—
and then stirs within that child as the uncreated
     light which has cradled it
and remains its home in the world, the power itself which sees
     and neither rages nor faints.
The sternness of justice? That too the witnessing luminosity
     surrounds and effortlessly carries.
Effortlessly: *virtù* is the strength not prior to but encompassing virtue.
     It is not the breath,
and not the lung either, but bright space, timespace,
     straight through that British night meadow
to your New Jersey rooms, your rooms and then mine,
     straight on into the retina
of your Virgil fainting because too many faces appear there,
     and into the eyes of me and
my fellows where the Arab and Malay do not really appear.
     Through either kind of whiteout,
searing or oblivious, equally the path of justice.
     I salute you. Pray for us.

A Metal Denser than, and Liquid

What sets the worst architect apart from the best bee is this: the architect builds his structure in imagination before he erects it in reality.

—MARX, *Capital*

Had he sat there, a witness?
at Posen, the speech in which Himmler
spoke the abomination,
a darkness within darkness.

He tried to believe he had not.
There was enough in him
that he had to go on living.
And so he would not remember.

There had been talk, briefly,
of his being made successor.
Before the complexities.
He didn't talk about that.

Then there was the hospital,
when he had nearly died
from the task and the unspoken.
No one did that task better.

Doing it better became
his way of foxing the wolves
who pranced around him. But
how much had he taken on

else, and where had it led him?
He worked from that bed till he broke.
Then lift-off, out of his body:
light, rich appointments, warm colors,

the doctors did a ballet,
and at last, there at last
he felt for his wife how much,
he smiled the withheld, he fully

was who he knew he was
and knew he could go. But was sent back.

His prison chaplain, although
supposing the story might be
fantasy, knew it came with
the urgent stink of Lazarus.

Ach it was all in his mind
laughed Frau Speer. If only
she too could have seen it:
he'd nearly found the exit

from his squeeze, he'd skirted
the suck of the great change.

   And one of my own tribe: when
transferred for interrogation
to Versailles, what saved him
was an English parachute major
taking him for a drive
to Paris.
         We went through

St. Germain and Bougival
where in years past I dined
with Vlaminck, Alfred Cortot—
then we walked along the quais
and looked at the stalls. I was
horribly sad, but I bought
a print like any tourist
and—so silly—it made
me feel human.

   And if I briefly abhor
this fantast while pitying him
the hole in his feeling, with
art as surrogate—if
his uncontrollable falseness
even to himself, the untracked
changeability,
alarms and disgusts me?
                              Then
somewhere near right here
I have lost the treasure
of shaming accuracy
about myself.
                        His decades
of fox-introspection
kindle several days
of fascination and
gnawing discomfort and
discernment in my corner,

while a voice both sharp and soothing
intervenes: *discernment*
is not judgment!

                    May it
be so. But this rankling rawness?

Cicero did not warn us:
Aesop makes tricky reading.

Art is not surrogate,
but the gate. The gate stands
to be passed through. The passage
is to truth truly lived

whatever the means, however
mean, for what is great
and shines quiveringly is
self-presence from the soul.

    Where the treasure lies
there lie the means also.
The metallurgist's kit
went with the gold galleons
to the bottom. Divers brush
scum from lakes of it there,
push at it, play with it,
quivering mercury—

a comeliness past that
of gold, because it lives,
a mirror to the will
to undergo all change.

Unloved, the master in him
went seeking a mad attachment.

Suddenly undersea,
the day, the room, strangely
rich in appointments, when evil
seems to shake far beyond me.

Mirror, mirror, on the floor,
which beast in me shall I adore

judiciously?
                    May his rootless soul
have felt, somewhere, compassion.
Let compassion rise
and quiver in me. And let me
turn again to the sun.

Barges at Koblenz, 1986

The terrace where potatoes, sweating beer,
tables where vinegary production,
shelve out gradually to night and grow there
while the hill fortress rides in Kliegs—the terrace
where supper and the generations also
are served, reposes after effort, after dulled
memory and gathered disquietudes
have sat to eat and maybe to have it out
or maybe not, but at all costs to eat,
and listen for legitimacies of the age
from diesels with running lights: low because laden
heavily, laden because our animal needs
hold constant.
                From my shoemaker ancestor's day
through the catastrophes, one heavy pulse.
With grace I'll recollect wet pilsner chill
in my hand a decade hence and dip in the dark
hum again, asking: What was it for, construction,
and will she, my child, and will they, her children, will all
inherit? Will the lawyer's theological
exactitudes, his nasal angelisms,
penetrate this soughing sloshed ground-bass,
cutting through swirls that take the diaphragm
for their meaty ear? And what will he read out?
Surprises, let us hope, in distribution
and novelties in the mad bequest. They tug

predictably up through vineyards on the Moselle,
slide down to the larger centers. Their bulked crisscross
stands visible only when red dot sweeps green
above a subdued cadence of tympani,
and I think: Not for this was the Pastor hung
nor the manifest end of things elided.
Unholy peace from throbbing quiet, bow waves
shoving inshore the litany of this place.

At the Atom Plant near Vernon, Vermont

Down through groves where a chief
ceremonially spoke,
then memoryless roofs. Once path,
now road—but the way that broke
in our hands questions hands,
its heavy release your sheaf
of stony shapes, their ends
contained. And the rest is wrath.

This people is offended
not so much by your squat
poise over danger as
by any reach extended
through resonating profiles,
echoing diction and thought—
it hears otherwise, a glaze
of motions, rough blank bliss,
no Bradford or Herakles
moving through smash and blunder
into continual
shearings of bonds in your piles,
moving in forms of the harms
soon to havoc themselves
in froths of rampage tall
on a graph's shoulder. This

nation will not pass under
the bar of judgment, it sees
itself in singular terms.

I have absorbed from damp shelves
of grass where the heron waits
then lifts off, your stack, block,
and tainted hum, I have watched
the graded evenings walk
their cloaks over you, subtle
lengthenings of the fates
then trimmings of them, notched
seasons at the throttle
of that curve—and have tried
to add no slightest grain
to the perception, to pull
the rest of it back, even, through layers
of sheen curling on the mulled
dusk river that lift, divide,
vanish. To uncover again
the submerged balance, its powers.

Transmission Lines

to E. G. B., visiting after ten years in 2001

At first I did not remember the tree's name,
although in the next moment it arrived:
locust. And in that lacuna the white blossoms
came on in magnification, making whiteness
all through me, and a breathlessness although
I could breathe. That was later, however,
when naming a poison and extracting it
came on as the task. And for that came the blossoms
and you, not in person but as phantom,
cleansing some reek of the ground. A keener friend.
Essential, there, that you not speak, and that I
not greet you, only half-knowing where I stood.
    Like someone tailing a wayward charge, your figure
trailed mine as I left a high hall. As ever,
your straight-hearted love of the Greeks pushed through
silences. I had just filched from discards
on the floor—cast-offs from a rummage sale—
the applewood plaque of a knoll in the Capital.
Not quite Washington: rather, the inmost
node of the republic, less white, more vast.
A bas-relief rose from rolling meadow—a naked
hero with a younger man, guide with ephebe—
standing in acres of inane green.

With no one.
Whom was this meant for? Isolated, half
memorial and half instigation,
with only the air of pastness: the present prickled
through it from the boy, with fresh reports
coming down from there that leaders intend
to winnow the troubled ones from the schools, the kink-links
out of the chain (somewhere they're meant, sotto voce,
to check out of here, do each other in,
or do themselves in). Not that the includers
have not been dogmatic themselves, progressive yet
pressing down hard. And not that I jack myself up
for backing victims against victimizers,
Galahad against the screws! They are as old
in this mood as the first settlers, and as grim
in settling with it. The programmatic includers
and then the backlashers: lost between them,
a child with a book.
                        Yet the carving gets it right:
disrupters are potential heroes—twice-born,
abandoned on hills and shoved adrift in wicker,
raised by the miller and his barren wife,
runts of the gods waiting to range outward
at some risk. The reach-me-down shortcut
that cannot get them there is doing drugs,
yet at least they reach. Masters of initiation,
to ram them down the paths, past images, until
the heart stands free of them all—where are those people?
Not that asking the question will excuse me.
Nor will my muttering that the economy
of wish and squeeze, which even the managers
cannot manage, is out in front of us all
heating the pavement to pudding. That path, that, too.

Leaving, I saw that I was again on campus
near my beginnings.
                    So the lessons were not to be taken
personally: your silence underscored that.
Dim dignity for the old! And for the young
smoldering, half-ignited, this. Just this.

   Applewood, color of a rusty dawn,
who will distinguish cold nerve from loss of nerve?
In the little carved scene, muscle rivers
down the whole form, a relaxed calming fist
beneath a focused but wide gaze. No split
anywhere in the flesh, for a great river
builds on mucked beds, the great builds up from grunge,
depth hangs from breadth and basis. But if fathers
give their young to triage they take the mirror
from their own faces, the higher thus building
cracked on the lower thing hustled away,
thus to totter. Not immediately,
and may be not in the manifest places of blood.
Mr. McNamara, there's a phone call for you
said a small man on the ferry to Martha's Vineyard
two years after the war. They walked outside
into the night, around the pilothouse,
and then the painter, fury claiming him,
whose brothers went to 'Nam—one later a general—
whose uncle was an admiral, whose cousin
was a major in the Marines, this painter swung
the head of the World Bank over the railing and pitched him
towards the tail-race, but skier McNamara
clawed his fingers into the mesh like a gecko
and clung there saying nothing. As he had for years.
And refused to press charges.

Nothing shook him as that did.
That unpremeditated avenger reared
his decorous cleanly bearded non-weirdo grip
from the swish black of the crossing and heaved out
once into the split before he was grabbed
from behind and flattened. Heaved much as rage climbing
a CEO—or a letch rashing the privates—
or the impulse to embezzle—will bridge divisions
by crushing them together or pitching them
into stern-slip through the propellers.
                            The split builds back
from the low thing. A cultural runt, mere painter,
possessed by the whole responded from more than he was
into the unbearable to jam them close
and get them, one *tremendum*, off all our backs.
I wouldn't say I hate the guy at all.
You get a chance at one of those people, right?
You're out there. Maybe the chance will never come back.

   And this time Laios was recognized at the crossroads,
the father who in his panic had deep-sixed—
so he thought—an abomination, his deadly child.
Yet this time not even his own boy: a stranger, blank
confronter: so many sons. . . .
                      The biographer
of McNamara developed not one but five,
seven, a dozen lives in order to get that single
un-self-disclosing man. A bag of lives,
of lies, of lay-by captures from all sides, across
race, class, ocean, surmise, scooped facts, rhymed times,
a such-and-deploy operation with the bag
still hungry and leaking.
                      No, dear Suetonius,

not twelve big stinking fish. No: kaleidoscopic
polybiography, until the last
peripheral Joe, even the pair of long-haired
COs in my Princeton rookie's office,
ephebes walking away from their garrison duty
and so, like me, never put to that proof,
even we extras showing up on the set
as collateral sons, with depositions, blood tests,
lineups, and oaths.
                    The split builds back and on.
For those who went, one aspect of themselves
stayed here to be hunted down, and cradled, and birthed.
For those who did not go, that same aspect
indeed went over there, to get hurt, and die
a little. Some of those who stayed here
catch themselves now thinking they went there, even
that they fought then came back and stood in the fight against it,
Philoktetes clearing his wound both ways.
One friend who stayed, feeling more shame than clarity,
thirty years later came to see that his natural
root and his gift and his anger had done a tour
of duty there, and got wrecked, and now demanded
his full attention, disruptive and fussed, urgent
to come home at last.

                    And now, friend, your visitation.
Your Pindar, your Mithraic converts to Paul,
your Homer, hanging back with you at ten paces,
are curious—a little—to see what I'll do.
Anger prolongs life in some. In me it kills
the chance for meetings, and this is one of them.
A meeting, though, in this non-place specifically
sited, a phantasm grommeting into

my old campus, the hour stained like a slide
swabbed with the red smear of the twenty-seven
cities that went up in that summer of
a refocussed civil war.
                          The most retarded
of the advanced peoples, the most parochial
of the gleaming cosmopolitans—what sleeping
hugeness, of what age, required all of that
to stir us! Now a resumed slumber dismisses
the wound-bearers, the key-hiders, our blunt babes. . . .
Not that people can't count, or do the numbers
again and cry out, chalking in demonstrations
of what figures and which of the numbers will crunch
to some effect.
                  My own demonstration?
It was May, and locust phalanxes bloomed
white in a stilled cascade. Forty years on,
I'd learned that the World War Two family story
of noble death was scrim for a shame whose pain
had them choose a good lie. But their mistelling
had clouded my background senses. Subtle disturbance
and the lie both flared palely into view
and hung from the foliage of decades, the disturbed
dead man who'd have been in his seventies rising
to claim his facts. Less than the swung clusters
of flowering chestnut, locust offers on drooped
leafage its open arrays, the least glamorous
of the flaunters. He needed to be heard.
To know that his guilt was bearable. To bear,
not as the leader he became but as youth,
his whole spread, and stand from his tortuous root.
A man who kills himself for a common failing
shatters a floorboard in the house for those

he has lived with—which their lies won't cover;
they sharpen its edges. He could not speak, and they
would not speak straight, and so my own speech grew
muffled, thrashing through veilings. Disruptive
not in some schoolroom, but insidiously
and to myself. He needed to come as he was,
father, officer, and brief sexual betrayer
but most the worker of his gift for yoking
the young bull in his linebackers to one thing,
to the best thing, beyond sullen violence.
Seventy-some in a coach's mud and captain's
blood-caked jacket, the young in the old, standing.
So he too waits, with you.
                              The very old
and the trashed young for a flash seem to me
hermits unintentionally proliferating,
indecent multiples of gauche dignities
impeding the flow, damming it everywhere
with the saving obstacles they themselves are.
A bizarre intuition of the actually
fruitful facts? But come down, come, to the case:
will it notch me towards the first end of man,
bugling Taps? *dulce et decorum est*
pro patria, but the sweetness buds as sweat
from us both: I don't want his burden, and he
doesn't want those long brass monosyllables
in his young-old face. *Don't cut your thread!* Even
my screamed instinct must line the unspoken the way
the unspoken lines being.
                              Protest past anger
stills him and he seeks elsewhere, after the by-blow
not-altogether-wrathless father, truth,
or his truth, as he showed me in that parade

of white epaulets down the leaves, hanging garden
seeking its self-denied ground at long last.

    And you have sought me.
                        It's as if your mentors
wait for inventions knowing we know the case.
    Maybe because your Greeks are half-Japanese,
and wouldn't have envied our cities, or us, or our chances
given the chances we thin out at both ends of life,
hermits are what come back to me: a footnote
about the Japanese monk who broke his seclusion
after a long stint of stilling himself, to seek out
animal warmth once more. This time, however,
he is my straying self-killer, and he is
also those tribes of teens and codgers, rejects,
and I am him, and them, ensemble the body
our gray poet intoned—he, the loneliest
except for Miss Emily—as the symphonic
dawn of inclusives, the light of a gregarious
vast east self-renewing, comrades of dawn,
Greek, Japanese, craze-gifted Dutch, *plat Deutsch!*
I-he-they sally into glades
of well-spaced trunks canopying meadows,
which the first colonists blundered into along
the southern coast, the deer-parks they left in Europe
handed to them here by the burn-hunt-and-plant
land management of the tribes.
                        Only the trees
able to grow through and above those fires
welcomed the invaders.
                        And when I finally
locate two of my own kind in those glades
similarly posted in aloneness, and greet

the first one, he mutely raises his fist—
and then the other one, he too raises his fist.
What I'm supposed to say is canonical:
What's the difference? which of course has either
no answer or a commentary on answers.
Instead I turn to acknowledge you and those
Sophoklean presences. I know that you won't be
staying that much longer. I say to myself,
They inscribed the young man's title, kouros, to name
the ageless who stand it and go on, initiates
capable at the limits even in age,
striders even on an elder's pins, elders
newborn in scope for the straight thing untampered.
Veterans seared fresh by the real. And I say to you,
This is our one chance to exchange greetings,
and lock eyes with all of you as you fade into burnish
on the air, the betrayal of children, and white trees.

Single Wing

Twirling by the beach-squatter's house, bright socks
   and tubey flourescent banner
and pleated spinneret pink, orange, green—
   one palette for the glory.

Microscopic from the wave surge
the cycles creaming upslope,
blanchings sinking to a buff blush—
a rank reek clears the head
so gurgles can insinuate the mix
Tod und Wiedergeburt, und Wiedergeburt—
   where is the language for it?

   A vast dodderer in his gums
murmuring like the horde against Moses because
he has coughed up from his first pastures the cud
set aside by forty years of professing
   expertise and good sense.

   The day I fell down a well back of all tides
came black contentment unlooked-for, and time's other—
and the other palette for the glory.
I did not know, then, the coastal town where Parmeneides,
Greek in Italy, gleamed from the sea then arrowed
caves to suspend himself,
untorchable in the dormitory, surrendering ignition

to unlighted light.
    Pholarchos, Pholarchos, lair's lord,
cave musterer and master, usherer
into a blotto interregnum, where
 is the nerve for it?

 No antagonist to crank it to drama.
No less than the whole breathing of life hung stilled
without the splash of enemies or dominion
or gain to crown it.
    The irritant of this moment,
plumpish road vans that burn more and kill harder,
headlamps relentless—and out-of-sight caves pumped with brine
to extract the black lees, the entire setup
soon to torch out like a blown wellhead—my profligate
tribe's newest toy bug-eyes the bouncy
access road and then rev-stops. Yet it is not,
they are not, the antagonist. They make part of a wave
that rolls under the entire mix, towards a glory
whose outcome is unforeseeable, and so
contempt does not boil in the heart
but seethes in with a following wind and whitens.

And is not contempt but a fierce inter-sensing.

Follow the legend of the blood-drabbled child
born when the Temple was razed and you trail the cabalists
through their legend of the Two Messiahs, Messiah ben Joseph
becoming both the Suffering One and the Opponent. . . .
 So, bored failed hunters versus myself growing
bigger than myself?—none of that is this outerness
of feeling, or non-feeling, that combs and froths and slides in

to sink away and leave the drained yet refertilized
unexpected.

        For, bigger out of late grays,
a swept-wing vagueness at first
leaned in and up, as a pompadour
flings from a tenor's brow in stage lights yet faint also
as that shine dims:
                bigger and misting black,
seed of a squall from the lung
of coincident non-feeling, wetting the non-bride
of the solid-in-vacancy world, for
stone is spirit, spirit stone: between them this fluent
margin with fuming crashings deep beyond sleep.

And then was gone at a height of eighty yards
exhaling.
        I would ask them to join me,
the dear ones, if I could find it again,
the mouth of that lactate blackness and peace.
But it found me. I would lead them down
to bounty.
          Where the second sun, at home there,
remembers itself over our sea
rocked to loosening lacework among stones
under a trembling line of geese.
                  World is one action
meeting no antagonist: the action is single and self-emptying and
where is the measure for it?

Magnolia Beach, Massachusetts, August

III

Conus Marmoreus, Night Piece, Rembrandt

in memory, Clarence Erwin Peck

Scrolled like Torah's wealth speckled with turtle armor,
shell protruding from shadow, its mouth wider as
the trim cone tapers: finally as gift the obscure
repository for my father's transparent alchemy.

Track star and ice-wagon teamster with Spanish-looking fiancée.

At the next turn of the shell he runs after the platform
on the last car of a train sliding off into snow.
Grasps at the railing, hauls himself and his bag aboard,
staggering to his berth. Mill stacks behind vomit blackness.

No past can hold him now, he burns through.

The one that might have held him, Louis Bromfield's farmstead,
engaged only his lesser demon: a broom handle
for planting tomatoes! His fingers manipulate molybdenum
duds in the barrels on foundry floors while he calculates.

Gantries slide overhead to muffled tympani then crawl.

I stood with him there, so felt his fire: the privilege denied
to many sons was mine, he showed me his métier—

cleaner than Johann Becher's at the Bavarian court,
where alchemist stage-manager *Naturphilosoph*

stood crossroads entrepreneur changing the diapers on science—

no, not the Holy Roman Empire, the American:
and within that, anomaly: for he, who could have taught,
or gone to the top, chose neither so that he might invent
from within the jell and spurt in alloyed iron's lattices.

Finding no outward vessel for his heat, he secretes one.

Builds vessels that will treat the metal that will jacket
world-weapon, that will sheathe the ticking abomination.
Nacreous gristle at this turn of the shell shines
yellow then solar, and a swarthy Bessemer pours.

Then shields for reactors on the submarines. Cold plastrons!

From a horse-drawn ice wagon, in fifty years. Something more
than acceleration marks the marvel: it is service
to his day's decent hope all innocent now, in a devout
descent, furnace glow while cold fathoms engulf him.

The Juggler before Our Lady, all night in the crypt tossing.

The gleam around that figure they say kept the sexton
from clearing the little craftsman out of there, nor
would I think of disturbing my own at his card table
under a late lamp, no cult image smiling down.

That speed-up? not the point. Time outruns no river.

Slow to lift to its surface blobbed impurities
which themselves pulse and glow in crusts on its lake, ardor
so core and speechless. Trusting from the floors
of seas the starbursts elder and endless he taught long love.

How long, sweet man, to know your nature. How long that sweetness.

The externals of this house, which from one point of view
unroll the codex from its cardiac stem, have glistened as
aggregates of the aeons, many in one, at a depth of
seventy atmospheres. And this shall be a sign unto me.

San Andrean One

Clearness and surf
beneath the evening Venus
and to hand, one rinsed pebble,
scriptorium of genesis
and the spilled bearing
of a great wheel,
filmy with Pindaros:

Undying, the gods
deal deathward men two blows
for each blessing.
Fools waste them both.
The best make both work for them,
folding pain in,
raying the light outward.

Scanning time for the second,
I honed the rim of Pacific
while behind me
friends and their children repiled
char-sealed
carbuncle-cored logs
near wine: a Viking's pyre,
but that stone,
since I was a young fool
and therefore to meet

Parzival's parade
                    of glowing marvels
             scripted the first time
for error, I lobbed far out.
                    Grace and power
             of a second blessèd chance!
             Skittering splash
aft of sunset, sprayed bowsprit
             for our beached fire ship,
                    wine in the evening
             with mock toasts to Grendel.

             It is more than memory
             of error, of evil,
                    which inserts cure,
just as it is more than
             event which stands eventual.
                    Unfolding in both,
             a double design.

             Matter awake
      cries it as character,
             sheer river of the mass
             hums destiny,
      but see light climbing in each
             to meet the other,
to focus the second, their mingling.

      One such second: the crypt
             of Alberti's gem
             in January
mists, Mantova's gut-cramper,
      San Sebastiano stays sealed

in haze needing
a second penetration.
Faint sunlight,
rows of the regimental
ensigns, tattered,

miniature on their standards
over the mute roll call:
Ethiopia, Albania,
Greece, Toscana.

Alberti's Rome
over the felled ranks,
compact basilica
miniaturized for that
stilled convoy,
dust dribbling
down the tricolors.

Messer Batista of the Alberti,
jested Lord Gonzaga
his protector,
who knows what he has made for us;
church, mosque, temple?
—on a central plan,
its walls drinking from the wet ground
like wicks or straws,
and so he wedged
a windowed crypt beneath
and between them,
an air conditioner
staffed by the useful dead.
Alberti, who knew

Florence as Florence knew itself
              not, returning
       with his exiled family,
emending and crimping and pruning the prose
       of the nobles
              for *pochi scudi*,
       the first blow exile
and the second penury.
              So his pocket basilica
       comes also from frequenting
the cordwainer's, the smith's junk shop—
       for what they did and how
              they did it, he *looked* at.

       Yes: look into those ways—
              metal against stone
                     became the edge
              against the neck
of entire continents, the tribes:
              Maya, Oglala;
       Java, Ethiopia.

       I know his type:
              not Parzival
       but Cologrenaunt, wayfarer,
inventor quietly grinning:
       not content to survey
only, but cribbing from craftsmen,
       looking. Grinning and taking.

       Some second gaze, then,
       to unseal from dumb cold
              holding the expelled breath

his chapel beached
for how long on the reef
        stretching from Augustus
                to the Boss, the boor—

Alberti's architecture
                cleanest of the grand
at times seems to administer the blow
                which itself seems
        unending. My stone
                lobbed into oncoming
        waves to break that spell?
        but the sand where
                even then I stood
                        comes from poundings
        of waves elsewhere,
                if space utters
these paradoxes. Combers
        over my own shoulders.

        Reb Hile Wechsler
                saw them swelling,
piling in from the rim.
                Taking the name
        Jaschern milo Debor,
that is, the pastureless
                straightener, *Yashran*,
he published dreams
his mentor and superiors
                discretely shrank from.
                Only the poets
        anticipated him,
                one with red cloud

drawn black to the evening mountain,
and long before that
the Black Cloud of *Y-H-V-H*,
the same that would shroud
Jesus on Moriah,
with Peter gibbering
about cobbling together
some tabernacles.
Inside its folds, its bowels,
twistings that go past pain,
marriages inconceivable
to mind, there they
convolute their matings,
there the two lights
make coitus,

and so each bearer
of mingled luminosities
to our kind
must harrow a piece of the field
with an agony
from which there wobbles a bright
ignored lamp.

Doom for the Twelve Tribes,
the reb saw it
sweeping its cumulus
up through the Germanies.
He had been felled
by illnesses,
he dreamed also
that his little son
would survive

a hard birth, but then
paired sicknesses got the infant,
        the second one bringing
    death's dream signal
        at last to the father.

    From this he knew:
        no secrets,
the weird visions must go forth.
        They went unread.
    Israel Torres
with troops in the New Mexico waste
        found a stockade of ghouls,
    and another dogface
        sent closer to ground zero
to fetch men from a bunker
            smelled them burning,
then saw one clawing at electrodes
            coming with blood
        from all the gates of the senses.

    We can neither confirm
    nor deny what you saw:
the generals to the witness.
        A second time
    is not necessary
        for the primary,
            the ineffaceable.

But with Goetz, as with Wechsler,
    we may see it
        before it is quite here:
When the cloud did not budge

its weight from heaven,
and in the peoples the sun
was snuffed out,
then the deep light
came close,
sleep told us: You are here!
Your white form
cries out into the radiance,
wave on wave,
we are never old!

Let it be noted also
in credit to Victor Weisskopf,
his eyes lit at Trinity,
that when the fireball
blossomed over the desert
and a blue halo
manifested around
the yellow-orange sphere, he remembered
Grünewald's
Christus lofting out
of the catafalque, over the crumpled
soldiers, yellow-orange
body-aura
afloat in a blue halo—

let it be noted
in the darkroom illumination
of a developing X
that the painter
had embodied more than
the lysergic-acid
hypersimilars in grain-rot visions

of the lazars at Isenheim.
That the bomb exfoliated
the wheat bud of oppositions
        in an unscripted Eleusis,
Messiah one with the Beast,
    which Mathis held up for us
        someday to get to.

Never old! And nevermore
may we be quite so young.
    My boyhood stands
beside a Hungarian
        machinist with mangled hand
    who sang to his junk pile,
Beauty-full Iz-lee of Nowhere!
        Beyond it, fields
    planted with celery for
        the favored goulash
and paprikash, rabbits
        in a wire warren,
    then the pastorals
        of charred slag.

        Ours is the world
    in which conceivably Alberti
        would have tendered him
    a look-in, yet over which
        the Iz-lee of Nowhere
gathers to fall in resentment—
        the payback, the second.
    Time to retrieve
the heaved pebble—to reverse
        spray inward

upon the calyx of splash
and thereby raise
back along its arc
the stony illegible.

How dark spores
enter us. How they burn through!
When the man nudged
past the divine threshold
by the gray goddess to eat
with those powers
was still here, not incinerated,
he shot fire shafts
into the cave at Lerna,
drove the snake out,
and with Iolaos
seared shut eight of the necks
with flaming tree trunks
so their heads would not redouble.

This let him come
untouched to the center,
the ninth and deathless head.
On the road leading
out of Lerna to Elaius,
in a pit there,
he tamped it down with his bow butt.

The serpent, death.
Though he would slay his
own children, this thing
was accomplished, but with the stroke
of negation, not the capture

of the unseizable.
A stone's dive, *sssst*, below sundown,
after which
in the cool trill of descent,
its oscillations
of black concentrate
against buoying deeping green,
a light is not scattered
but sealed home.

San Andrean Two

At our door in his gas mask
        because of pollen,
the landlord checking on my pruning
        of the acacias, an entire orchard
            around our cottage—
and he asked: had we seen the bridgework yet
                on the moon?
a cottony booming through that mouth mesh,
        thence to the UFOs
definitely more frequent at dusk, and on freeways
        they nudged his bumper twice.
        The inventor
of a hanging soap-cake gripper, saucer-like,
        bought out by the soap makers
        because it saved too much soap.
No, we had not seen those bridges. *Well keep on looking!*

Behind the cottage a streambed
        followed a finger
    of the San Andreas Fault.
A corrugated steel drain half the height of a man
        began there, running beneath
pastures around the dark amber SYNTEX drug headquarters
        to the emery-board Veterans' Hospital,
            prototype for Kesey's
    One Flew over the Cuckoo's Nest.

Through the dry weeks
stragglers in gray pyjamas came from the hole, straightened, blinked,
and scuttled off.
That grove of acacias, pastures,
and hills dotted opposite with Live Oak now couch villas
redundant among redundancies,
Los Altos Hills, L'Escuela School.

Those hills rose directly over our grove, the forested Coast Range
where a self-appointed citizen militia held its maneuvers,
one of whose members snapped my portrait
as I turned the engine over
on a cold morning—*Hello there!*—then ducked and ran off.
Mornings until eleven
fog rolled over the crest and hung in wide, stopped waves,
a vast Elvis pompadour
draping the brow of the rampart,
half-Japanese through trees, the ocean's calm look-in, mist of divinations
undivulged, coiled smoke
over the tripod of the Bay's rim. While Kenneth Rexroth's nasal
complaint from the radio turned to gurgles—the mike
for his review of *Science and Civilization in China*
having slipped into his bathtub—I would look up through our trees
now gone at those trees going into whiteout.

When Turullius, one of Caesar's murderers, clear-cut
the groves of Apollo Cyparissius,
where the god's mortal son Asklepios received cult,
it was to build the fleet
for Marc Antony and Cleopatra,
and so Octavian put paid to Turullius. The medico
revenged by a field marshal!
Asklepios

got to be so good at his job that he raised a dead man
        and also had to be put away.
           I met my medico
in the Stanford graduate dining hall, the Drofnats Mess,
        Lucien Kabat, Manhattan Luke,
who married a black woman and went to Mississippi
      to replace Mickey Schwerner after Chaney, Goodman, and Schwerner
        got killed in the campaign

to test the Civil Rights Bill, and while Luke was still cramming
        for his Medical Boards.
His mimeoed blur-blue weekly letters piled up under the yellow
        pungencies of the acacias.
At a long table with an engineer who bunched three tall paper cups
        into an inverted array
and rotated them against each other, saying, *The consequences*
    of this little move can get you a Pee Aitch Dee,
      we had admired the bosomy
        carrier of a milk pitcher
among those tables, designating her the reincarnation
    of Delacroix's *Liberty Leading the People*—and she was,
Johnson's domino men prosecuting their jungle war and we
        convening in Redwood City
to march to the napalm shipping point, cordoned
      by fellow citizens with baseball bats.

Jugs of milk, full tender breasts, and leering candidates
      for a millennial initiation—
we needed more than three conical, mutually sliding surfaces
      to gear us into engagement
with powers that might resolve all that emerged in us then.
     And to see past worship of the feminine as answer—
      an attractive turn, indeed most needful,

yet Robert Graves's regiment
and all the hod-carriers for the goddess
would resurrect Carthage, renew the blood at Çatal Huyuk.
Two, they are, the breasts' aureoles, and ovaries,
but single the light past them.
Bilateral symmetry in our form, towards the unity of the city.
And two-ness finally springs an arc there—
Demeter and Athene near the fallen,
their corpse tenderness tensed:

the mother of Persephoneia in piety towards harvest,
reclaiming the dead to bury them as august
fertilizer for *foisson*,
over against ramrod Athene, burying in order to plant
a crop of wrath, sprout the knives of vengeance
in counter-harvest to the grief mother's.
Breasts reaffirmed in armor,
her occult child a serpent nursed beneath the Acropolis, issue
from a sporting try by sweaty Hephaestus
whose spurt fell short
but splashed, so that Athens' future sneaked up-thigh from the splatter
thence to coil near milk in the dark.
If each of us is a conversation, that conversation gets mothered here,
between tears for a gone daughter
and a blacksmith's hard-on, between the mourning that breeds corn
and plume-helmed love as vigilance.

The saucy charm of the androgyne in Athene's skirts? So many
dissimilar men love her:
the Chair of English at Drofnats, more corpulent than A. Hitchcock,
praised her to a stunned cocktail party: *We have*
three kinds of women graduate students:
the best are nuns,

then single women, then those living in the state of matrimony.
Between spells in the Meridian lockup Luke eulogized coworker Gail
who declined paying a fine for "a bad left turn"
because I do not owe anything for requesting service
guaranteed by United States law.
And so I will go to jail.
The convict-like loonies unstooping out of the storm drain
were Athene's boys, not her warrior dead
but the by-blow offspring kin
of her snake kid sealed away, probing underground.

P.f.c.s patrolling the fault line. And the Fault harbors
that tension between the two goddesses,
fixing its mounting strains
then slamming them loose, alternately contained and irruptive,
holding sorrow then blowing.
And that is the dialogue of civics, the goddess cure, if you please,
or even if you don't.
The nearby hills of dry Spanish grass and Live Oak embodied it
in a cattle herd: walking there
one afternoon we found them coalescing
slowly behind us, then gaining, then surrounding us. Standoff:
they demanded either that we leave, or that we answer
delphically perhaps:
Will we make it? Will the throat slitters spare us in the abattoir?
Moony chestnut eyes, milky intensities staking their claims
at a ton apiece.

Would resurrect Carthage, renew the blood at Çatal Huyuk?
No land is the Holy Land, for all are.
The mother in unity
would have each of us give birth to it,
me in my Hemlock swamp, the Pima in his desert, no blood feuds

over unreal estate—*will we make it?* Thus
from virginal light between the two aureoles, virgin birth
    as one's main task: only thus liberty leading the people.

A gaggle of actresses around us, a passel of turf-mad heavies
            they were not—
their grass had come with dray horses for the conquistadores
            and had outlasted the Missions.
    Silly-serious perhaps, but not negligible,
        the two mothers at one in them,
        the two wills to make death
    count most for life. Sway-sag uddered, and militant.
The civic tension is not to be resolved, but transformed, and it is not.
        Into that tension, the cow, or the medico—
    called back before his *floruit*, Luke waving from the precipice
            of that tension with mimeos—
diagnosing heart failure in the professional thief locked up with him,
    diagnosing his own cancer in the last exam on his Boards,
            reading the inflamed faces around his car
        near the Toddle House Diner, a waitress-Athene pointing him out—

the celebrated pointing him out at his funeral, but no one could say then:
            Already you have done your work,
                your stethoscope
took a full reading, you raised something in us that had died, and so
        the powers said, There goes another Asklepios, call him back.
Flashlights in your face next to a black girl in that car, and light
        fixing you where the Fault shuddered with dislodgements into
                the next reading of rest.
            I am happy to be back in Meridian.
We are very happy to have sat at your table. *I never thought*
            I would lose interest in politics—
the shield mother sent you in, and the wheat mother took you back,

and it is all right, you may lose interest in us too
         and we shall not mind.
You walked from the tunnel, you knew where you were, and showed us.
   My legs were shaking, but I managed to drive through the crowd.

      The first blow is struck by terror,
         the second by fear
on its way into the light, on its way through the tension.
      Only two energies for us, fear and eros
   with their spidery fault line. And so only the one tension.
     The centuries have cracked open,
the long hospital of Suso's *wolfish men* begins to disgorge its inmates,
   bigger crackings oncoming, jolting slidings past bigness
      and so who is counting—
a short Jew with his blood-pressure kit in a cold cell looks up
     and transmits Eckhart to me:
        there I was myself
and knew myself so as to make this experience man. Therefore
   I am my own cause according to my essence. . . .
     —*Not such a big deal*, he smiles,
     stubbing out his last cigarette.

Asklepian devotion? It was Sophokles' own cult,
   not only Sokrates' deathbed concession
      of a solar cock to healing darkness.
His plays administer the remedy: a long-incubated dream
      for the Athenian malady.
Self-rending Ajax is the general's heart-sore prescription
   of archival heroism for terminal ambition.
Luke neither read history nor found drama to the point.
      Yet his self-enlistment
     in a battalion of one was a doctor's,
     he swabbed his ideals with astringent

and numbered the smears,
going to ground in the same differential diagnosis
that inscribed Philoktetes and Tekmessa
as two grievers over one wound,
a queen city driven and deranged by its own light.

The herd moved in on us
as if it wanted answers—no flashlights, just milky insistence.
The strata have cracked open.
Well keep on looking! his masked head dwindling into the yellow boughs.
The ones who keep on looking climb out of the channel
in gray pyjamas,
keep moving down the fault line,
walking point for a platoon nowhere behind them.
They are apprehended. They are apprehensive. They are taken back.
It cracks open.
Closer to dusk, you see, they melt into the freeways, you'll see them then.
You can't stand pollen, buddy,
but you are a rare one for the war between the worlds,
which turns out to be
a matinee for the powers—
they glide in to take readings, they gather around and watch.

If I were to guess where the two Greek mothers became their own cause
according to their own joint essence,
and sat still for it,
and were seen as such by our landlord's gallery crowd,
it was in 'thirty-nine
when young Marguerite Yourcenar rowed out across Lac Leman
and bells started pealing
at mid-hour,
continuing, a bronze uncanniness over the water,
time booming into a bowl of space—

the war: and she guessed that, but waited,
for although I'd not yet been born neither had she come into her stream
                    but floated, hanging there
under the peaks on all sides. Older than crones, yet preconscious
                    that young woman, older than grievings
                    those concerted warnings

sucked into the upward abyss, cracking open into the peace
                    given to strain when it breaks.
                    No story there yet
and many stories ending, so in the vast bowl, question.
An angel ready to wrestle, but in the lake's deeps, or the air.
                    It used to be that to read things
        far off a woman would bend over a bowl of water and stare.
                    Yet to be a flake in the cup,
                broken din mingling from three shores,
        to sense the two nations and the five regions still present
                    yet suspended—
that may have been to bury it all as both fodder and knife,
                    to strew with a bereft hand
        and sharpen metal with a raised hand—
                the two mothers melded in her
                    to see all and know nothing.

And Sophokles' hymn to Asklepios was that of a priest
                    giving temporary shelter
        to that new arrival called *Master of the Hunt*,
                and the hounds go with him
                on a stone fragment at Athens,
and Luke, picked off like the god, tracked his hot quarry
                    in that chancy comedy
where he chased down rectitude and was hunted by yokels:
in his satyr play, word-painting his chorus of hairy ones,

Sophokles has them bay and sniff and even
    halloo like the hunt master, and so they shock the silenus
        who prays: *holy chance and daimon the tracker!*
            for when pack and point-man coalesce
        the rails twist and the tribe rides off scattershot,
        and then the one who drives the hounds is in me,
            and what shall I hunt, straightener and healer?

Well keep on looking. How utterly unscripted to see them,
    my mask-muffled Harpo Marx of UFOs
        and Luke waving from a cliff
            with stetho and mimeos—
        how unscripted the blessing.
And I am not ringed by the Alps. As a Pima shaman
    put it to a friend, about those who climb
            into the high places:
        you don't want to climb forever.
Yourcenar's vigilance in that moment of the blow: what is it but
        attentiveness for the second one?
Ours is the privilege, too, to hang in that vessel, oars shipped—
        the interval has been a large one,
            it began with promise:
America's troth between Greek-backed Europe and the Mongol-backed tribes,
    first the land bridge, then the bridge.

    A marriage proposed but never consummated,
            its brokers distracted
                by costly toys.
Circle of the genes and the winds, circle of household
            and cosmos-roofbeam,
        such the equipoise, the *dynamis*
            of an ever-shifting balance
        to be maintained, by Olympos

with Black Mesa—beneath the hotels
and the mining machines—Black Mesa with Olympos.
A drumhead's poise among all powers present and changing.
Among also the living and the dead! that greater
oikos, arching household.
The Pima, hearing *his* Asklepios whisper, applying *his* stethoscope,
and standing between the gateposts
of the two solstices,

heard them all as if climbing up and climbing down
at mid-year hunting,
two great packs in rotation, quarry incoming and seekers leaving.
A hunter welcoming the returnees is already among the dead.
They meet in the valley of the second blow
and marry, no longer alone.
Whereas the meeting here of the opposed communes has wanted fulfillment.
A step out into that exchange is the choice to die,
to hunt more than did Herakles with his main might,
not to hunt death but to die in hunting.
Not in the myth kit of our little Fausts! Yourcenar's dinghy bobbing
on the bell-rung membrane between mountains
floats among climbers who do not anticipate the limitless,
for the Greeks and young Wordsworth and John Muir
do not clamber forever. The shield mother and grain mother mingle
at halt. What shall I hunt?
The troth would be plighted, nor has it been,
the two streams from the two sources would crest in foam
over the jagged line running,
the ring would round on itself, at poise between the solstices,
their gate for our river—
the earth's crack opens beneath my stride
as the hunt itself opens.
My dead greet me and I would not climb forever.

IV

Carnival, Luzern, 1984

So, then, it goes only outward from us,
the dance? drugged and furry-winged, swarming,
and so reaches no root within stamens,
infiltrates no torse down a column, pressing
petals back to burrow in its own buzz?

(Blatting across the covered bridge
that burned later, trumpeters in platoons
reaming their brass through plaster rictuses
in yellow mountainous heads, they bobbed
under rafters daubed with the *Totentanz*.)

For the masters have taken listening that far.
Nothing half way for them: every alley
to its end, avenues past the allotments,
feet filthy with the raw gold they trail
from a blank wall, gutted warehouse, bare acre.

Even from night's halls, where at last their raids
are turned back, although they boast of stripped outposts.
Only when lights drilling through Fat Tuesday
spilled the full sex of color beyond even
those maskers, welling, welling, did I receive
hunger intact with its food, and horn, drum,

throbbing from the insides of things,
not rebounding as our off-rhythms and
tinkly refrains, and I grew heretic
from my tribe in that moment and was confirmed
when blackness swallowed the last band in peace
as they thrust drunken through the only gate.

Inkbrush Strophe and Antistrophe
for Juditha, 2000

Were it all
an inversion of obstacles—each
curb overturned—why, then,
you'd have stepped forth from your shadows
as the sole performer of your black tarantella
and our years, their lank willing
ciphers jigging in its wake.
Not a crowd, but quintessence.
And for sequence, the whelming simultaneous.
That much would have ponded your eyes, their curves
towards a last cataract,
behind them a Fifth Rome steeping
along canals, frontiers quaking
on their ripples, great gleam.
You would have spun, even, as the last prize
cast in the royal Hindu crapshoot, bride of five brothers
in the battle between worlds,
and would have trailed them through wilderness
so that they, and you, ripely lost,
might conquer.

But not so.
Your revisionist ambition, like
the era's invasive balm,
ointment of endings that would eerily shine

over shoulders of the epoch's bent demon
were it to stoop forth at last,
was to frame a garden
not a career, plough under
every microcrystal of the malady,
and plant yourself, each spoiler of your fate
farther off and drier
than posters curling
in some station corridor,
as mistress of enactments
of the aeons, a low table as cradle
for the crazed swish of justice swirled out
whole from a single charge
of your ink, wrists praying there, lifting themselves
into poise from the torn stab
of one stroke.

Porter of the Oar:

                                    the test for us
consummate know-it-alls would be to set out

our own sense of this figure where the coda blows thin,
where the spoor squiggles out into upland dust and stoniness.

From a whacked war to a modestly corrupt state,
returnee is what we'd call him, distinguished veteran.

Yet after the luminous bedchamber, this trek a ghost had laid
on his reduced essence. Hallucination, our medicos would chalk it.

After the long-meant reunion, this obedience to
unheard voices. From a whacked war to a woo-woo mission.

An olive tree rooted their marriage bed, yielding only to his
oak sweep. Did that oar thrust the olive farther, through the envelope?

Were he to lug it today, then how far inland? and when
would we blurt out our name for it? Terms termless now.

Yet first the point is not that he left again, but that his arrival
was delayed, for reasons of increase, Zeno's fattening arrow.

Then the point is that his oar, while remaining oar, was to become
something other in our eyes, and jolt us into speech.

The seas had come to stasis in him. So thenceforth
on would fold *in*, across the stable surf of hills.

Above snowline, peaks turning chartreuse. Multilanes stringing amber
down canyons and swallowed there. Futile dragonfly choppers.

Authority no longer spread for him from the air
shaping at three paces as she, prodder, protector,

nor in his shaping hands, but now in what they had welded,
salt to oak's grain white past the grape's candor.

From plugging his ears to giving ear to his own story, weeping.
From taking arms to being held by arms, soft, many—

at last he became woman.
                              Such the first phases, brassiere
as safe passage, dog's tongue as embassy wetting him onward,

none of it in the telemetries preceding him here,
or in his berserker rampage. Such codas make prelude.

The spook Badlands, northern Saskatchewan, only threshold,
deserts within the bluegrass and the corn, Sierra Madre without

guerillas and the hounding commandoes: even farther in.
We too would have to go there to be there waiting for him.

So for now he will get there first. The crust on his blade's
shallow scoop, invasion-silt then repatriation's,

will shine knowings condensed past these. The scan of his gaze
will chill and moisten, a guest go ungreeted, the one man

made one around more than man to go out past the one
and off the chart, off-limits with the pale and tasty

crystals of a long coming, savory after first bitterness—
this in the light there, standing, his sweep angling at poise

off that springy bulge above the collarbone, slanting towards
no hailings this time, no ceremonious inquiries,

but air, the accepting, the spacious:
                                        into which he heaves it,
awkward lance, floating with Zeno of Elea, psychiatrist of distances,

splitting the space before delayed impact into ever smaller
portions of entrance, the gates blinking faster for us.

Max Beckmann

Boundaries soldered or melted—lead congealed in stained glass,
or squidged into the muslin and flesh of ongoingness.

One parcel of existence rides pickaback on another:
if you came here looking for individual salvation,
you've got another thing coming, and it's coming from behind.

If a man falls, let it be through the blue vault
between structures a-tilt that presume not to fall,
that suspend flywheels of fortune near poddish air-boats
buoying creatures with wings. Question these, you're locked
in one of those buildings; fail to question them, you fall.

Nothing off-key, for it all squeezes into three adjacent rooms!
Boundaries go double-stroked across that squeeze, as across
the limbs akimbo on a military stretcher. If you came here
to get off the battlefield, you're not home yet, those incoming rounds
are the big draftsmen who rehung the windows and slanting doors.

Double-stroked, or smearing into shadow: the long study
of jeopardy goes double-breasted into alert ease
with cigarette holder. Shall I touch corruption directly in order to
titrate my immunity? Or shall I flee with kings on a raft?
While I collate my answers, and shred them, rooms heap up clutter,
but these same rooms also unpack themselves *lento cantabile*,
steamer trunks turned habitations, the pyramids' toy households

experimentally upended by the Berliner crack-up, hinting
in vain to their occupants in heavy mascara: the day will come.

We came in through one door but can no longer locate it.
And doors across the room, or in the next rooms, stand obstructed
by a swarming thatch of the bonkers and the smashing, both sets
more than themselves and less. Hero and tart trade gazes
but move toward separate exits. The air of voyage leaks in.
If you came here you will find many gates, many with faces and hands.
The air of transposition seeps in. Which door will you choose?

For the pressure pushed everything inside. Human lumber
has blown in from the explosion beyond these walls. If you
want out of here, you return to the artillery zone.
But also, if you go back out there, it will have changed
by virtue of your having done time in here, in fact
the world will have filled out to what you sought when you left it.
A psychotic flautist has been strapped to a dancer so that out here
the yoga student may pace unself-consciously.
Bird beaks have poked through surgeons' faces, reddened spikes
from the Mezozoic, so that in my room I may hear from the maples
calmly a finch and a jay.

Make one the other and I'm lost. Separate them and I'm done for.
So do I fudge the questions: wherefrom, whereto, which exit?
It isn't that he despised answers. He unpacked places.
Unpacking once into a storage stall, I halted:
in the next stall a cobra reared in gray clay, shadowy lily,
across from a dressmaker's dummy smoothly headless
floating at a window. The barn sheltering them
laned heavy planking around trap doors for hay, a ship's deck
from the eighteenth century. I stood, seeing.

The serpent was ready, the dummy was ready for showings-forth.
Between them passed an unreadable signal.

Renunciation is the first syllable of willingness,
Latinate pre-paving for the English of pre-yes.

   On the morning when from sleep I stood togged tightly
as one of the running monks on Mount Hiei,
with broad rolled hat and staff and jammed little backpack,
my kit contained the whole counterbalance for that hillside,
its web of trails spreading out and down from my feet,
and renewed, limitless air. The partitions inside the kit,
dark and superdense, intestinal, allowed now my entrance
into the incalculable and unmanageable system,
openness with paths, paths closing on themselves
so as to border always on the open. My stowed world
imploded that vastness and rode rightly. I could begin to move.

Little Ode on Wheat

Have I walked away from the great human beginning,
   our initiation into calm,
by turning from gluten and husk because they yeast to explosions
   through my inner workings?
No, from more: this barbed coif stroked and reddened your nape, Helen.

But the mass effect in its flamelets, and the broad mass of it
   smashing in wind, combing
back into braids there—to seek a single face, name,
   memory in that movement
is to mistake the world for the heart. Yet your joys, bread!

The mass of it: in the visions of seekers, one spear of it
   radiates from the unbounded
their rebirth. So the might of it throngs, meaning: one seed.
   But then, too, the mass of it,
for the masters of long time and the human aggregates,

freezes beneath a cold sun. Alexandre Kojève
   lecturing on Hegel in Paris
in the late 1930s, Kojevnikov nephew of Kandinsky,
   spellbound his socialist listeners
with Hegel Marxianized, his Hegel a hail on the wheat,

taking the argument on its face: one world and one knowing,
   and it is *our* knowing,

as it was this German witch doctor's, who heard Napoleon
    on horseback at Jena resolving
all antinomies. The absolute! and *we* know it,

and in knowing it we stop history, bring human process
    to cessation, apex . . . and yet it was
not Napoleon Hegel heard in the world's wheat, it was *Stalin*!
    And his listeners experienced ecclesia.
The rapture of abomination took them. My father's generation—

I must make peace with this fish-scale herb of peace,
    its nutriment of moons
uncounted, its flexing of bows that discharge no arrows, though arrows
    fly with the sound of a wheat field,
its power to hold great Adam in one place and nurse him.

The man on horseback on whose back the philosopher
    mounted to a gimcrack totality
was also a man many times head-over-heels off horseback,
    not broken but unlucky—
Napoleon approaching the Niemen to cross into Russia

went cantering through a wheat field on Friedland, or Marengo—
    their skeletons in museums—
when a rabbit tripped up his mount. They picked him up. They crossed over.
    Abiding there, the half-sibilance
of rusted hair lisping the seasons, centuries, pale wheat.

Eclogue

Back late to Boston. Or to Krakow in some other fate
that percolates up through fatigue? None the less, there are sentinels:
a raccoon has stopped mid-road, his close-set headlamps
wagering patience. I shut off the engine, then the lights,

wait for him to scurry plowdrift into shagged pines,
and sense the Quabbin Reservoir below them, miles long
over submerged towns, obols for this drink of peace. And sense
those whom I love far though close, sunk in heart-knowledge.

That fellow flashing me the alert is a keen eater,
feeling his prey in the water he reads the great exchange,
he stills himself over the vast bowl, levelly surveying
the rim between three realms—and what do I chew here, and drink?

For all is a feeding. The sweetest of it, and even across
the boundary of death, as transfer wakes taste
and soothes even the keenest rage. Because unseen mind
absorbs what the tooth consigns it, seen mind must see—

in Exodus the command came never to boil
a kid in its mother's milk, whereas in Greek Italy
Dionysiac priests indented that very menu into
gold leaves, for the initiations: *Drink not Lethe, but Mnemosyne.* . . .

The prohibitions fuel the releasings. Down one path
a young goat cannot, and down the other must, soak in the milk
of hot blackness, while between them hunches this little mask
with lamps and stripes, halting hoof, and gas pedal, and choice.

When it is stopped the soul sits startled yet tranquil,
its intelligence gleams in front of it and then vanishes,
branch-hung stars freshened out of unfactored age
beckon it to its end in renewed spaciousness,

so not this time, the bushwhacking, not this time the cold hand.
Nor the fat hand of praise. But into the black, out of it,
from its below, its above, velvet of it all turning,
the knowledge that I loved even through bunglings. It has come.

When it is stopped, the soul hangs then plunges into
connection that had not been there but now is,
a fluid medium, the alternately bright and black
lactose of benign dismemberment, floating

but aimed: the soul, stopping, at last is set to begin,
to drink in, look up, shoot through the archive of forestries,
reclaim its wilds but also churn the starter and slap
radiance over pine duff and burrow back into the world.

Little Testimony at Fruitlands, Massachusetts

A braid of black and white wools swings from my belt
for the monk Lobsang Gelek hung out to dry
because he lived sufficiently at liberty to speak
the name of his high lama—his nation occupied—

and because publicity the blind and many-handed
has dropped his rope in my hands, the sentimentalities
of mass fraternity steaming off, sun striking his cage
during my sleep so that waking in turn I may bless his.

Half the globe! No mimed or muttered exchange
that would know itself, belly loosened, as lived.
Belly tautened and loosened! Halfway between the pump
for blood and gut cradle, the coils no day leaves unmoved

if the penned body rides its river.
                                    And here from a peg
in one room, a freed going hung its gown: Shaker vermilion
    snood-pucker blossoming over the folded flow
of one jigging soul, its little sun at perihelion.

Midafternoon, while the monk Lobsang lay in darkness—
    I tried *The Twist* I had never mastered when younger,
    facing tall linen stained with raspberries,
shoulder with hips in a sideward slow leap through hunger

into my appetite: too long, now, the yearning
to mate within my movement the emerging bride
   even a monk holds close in sleep, and the longing
to thole my blood to its thrust out of gated swamp and glade

   into the unreddened land.
                          As it was meant to, out.
  For the terminator of light across shadow is rolling
a world back millionly outward, his room into mine,
mine into his; steadily a barrier is falling

   which his fate erected for him to thrust down
while still inside the walls of his keeping, and which mine
jiggles loose in the amorphous liberty
   of a mass advanced and retarded. Hymns to pain

long since choreographed flow behind both of us—
stronger meters master and choose us to push through
   what we have half-spoken or half-turned
shoulder to sacrum, to brave the break-point and go

with black to white wheeling on the boundary that glides,
scrub forest through marsh, past the homes of friends,
over our own roofs, into that rotation marked starry
even behind the light.
                  A cub sailor who aimed

straight for Aldebaran through the night watch
missed port but found his own direction. He did a slow twist
by ruddering fixedly. We may borrow shamanisms, like our troops
aping soccer among Germans after the armistice,

seeming generous, yet we stand vulnerable, defenseless,
nor is this steering by one's own star. The way
   out through the stars' vast body is through this body,
   confined flesh flying, the locked-up in ecstasy.

   I did not have to do what Lobsang did,
     no cell, no cess, nor loss of a whole people,
yet there is that in me which several times would have killed me
all the while I shielded others. So meet me, far one, to staple

   brotherhood here at the belt, tilting swirls
from your gowned pelvis, monk-cousin and rebel mate,
that I not go back on my birth, and rebirth, my death
to fixity; that my darkness braid substance through my light.

Ch'ang-fang saw the old merchant jump into his gourd,
then invite him in, his disciple, into the bounty
of cosmos. And I saw Doctor C. A. Meier in his age,
the Greek in his essays wrecked by a ham editor, squinty

and then laughing, say: *PIT-y! Mis-ter Asklepios—*
he was such a FINE fellow!
                    We had gone through the knothole
and yet, in that gravelly voice, spaciousness, and in what
could have been rancor, the rolling thing.
                          An unshadowed wheel

nudging me to the nova meant and marked from my origin
in fire.
        Voices arriving in this way score fire,
even the heron over my car dripping through takeoff
smolders with this beneath his buff blues.
                    So prison is for where,

in motion at last, I am fixed yet fly, *else a great prince
in prison lies*—flying fixed there to rot into the humus
of my preexistent freedom, to percolate its layers
    laid down by space and patrolled by the enormous

wing I am meant to wake to that out of and under me shears.

Rhyming with Davie's Sonnet in Mandelshtam's Hope for the Best

Evening flattens what morning lifted as sculpture—
can midday's slow arc be the sure location
of a white hope? Tracking those monumental
Carraras, we slowly topple, drifts and skewings
drag at us: endlessly over us, their river.
Bottom-dwellers, crawdads, we're not to fly
too far . . . yet so we must come of age, not with
fire but silt. For now sky rides in the earth,
its dizzying reaches—quarriers of marble
open a way, the worm's jaws are a-zing
with nebulae and the cycles, up the scarp
of a tiny peak within crawls my double, whirls
misting him; through them, valleys, orchards in
bloom, winking lakes with pike to be hooked and netted. . . .

A Stock-Taking

Inventoriable

A littel worlde made cunningly. Thus John Donne *en route*
from serving as attaché to Ralegh, then as secretary
to a power broker with brats bawling near his chair,
to holy orders—turncoat , unpolitic, a border-jumper.
And a narrow fashion over decades has vaulted itself
from Donne's erect effigy to Benjamin's self-murder in Port-Bou.

The shadow cabinet of the intellectuals, its premiership
nomadic, its secretariat faxing in from homelessness,
Graves on Mallorca a postcard pastoral in its eyes, chooses
the streetwalker who stays out late. Passaging is his anchorage.
Keener than they, he is disheveled as they would not be,
a Roman half-wall fuzzy on top walking, a Claudius

bemused that the day has made himself its street, signage
and unplanned interlocks waiting for his eye and tongue
to lick and love and then leave them, sharply bemused
that his self-evasion in knowing these things is an acrid
fruit cocktail of vocation without a main course
following. A privateer going to wreck gold-laden.

Gold no one else thinks to mine, shared out to the air
to gild and to gall. The uxorious man self-divorced.
A death-tax artist of sliding inheritances. Self-canceled
symbol of beast barters, their   X   his checkbook.
Here stood, for a moment, a man. Vacated into linkages
as the gone gods drifting in as smoke to choke or caress.

Like them he feels at large, yet in economies of the unmet
he may roll down a crack as micro-crumb, hunted rather
than big with the kill, dirty herdsman lost on his hillside—
and the wardens assigned this man to me as my double
because I veiled my center while they had fled from their own.
Even a stint with the Marines might not have broken the spell—

for the cannons at Cadiz left Donne merely fascinated.
For initiation inheres only in clearing away the planets
coagulated by false relations from a huge cloud,
so that sun, rising over the laundromat, may seat itself
among valid orbits, searing the near ones, pinging the cold—
each flake and wavelet on the new roamers attuned

in flux yet steadfast, poised before a condensed burning.

Walter Benjamin's Hope for the Best

Than the eucalyptus no taller, nor shaggier.
A fine scimitar gloss shines out from and through its leaves.
Than the spume off seawall no more insistent, no less erosive.
Let the agent that reshapes, let the power that stills, be

than the threshold no firmer, its gullies troughing our weight
through its own, *historia naturata*.

Painted a red clerk? wear black—painted a black, sink through the page,
as surf, glistening and spreading, whispers in.

On the bourse, in the arcade mini-mall, membranous exchange,
from cell to cell bright ooze, the pop of separation,
Its whole delight is in birth, the soul's happiness.
Than the wave's flush no greater, than the comber no swifter,
radiolarian in the fireworks burst, than its spread no wider,
its pulse a sheen over inky space.

If I see through facades into the girderwork, if I travel
the wiring to the turbines and furnaces, my eyes may tire.
I will peer anyway. If I shirk system-builders
and at the same time rehabilitate the traduced moods,
my friends may walk off. Let them go, vacancy
more deeply breeds change.

Stamped *arrière-garde?* Display the date of franking and say,
Lapsed address. The cave splashed with bison breathes sunrise.

Each lump on the forehead of a humpback, each nodule
shining as she crests through her bubble net to gulp krill,
raises a root mound for but one hair follicle. Which Hegel
would not bother to enumerate. Each is antenna
not for Jonah, though he passed her grapefruit-sized throat,
nor Nineveh, but the whole change.

Than the force gullet, than its flux tonnage, no other
mouth for my city. Our story is a herring school
to that milky keen cornea guiding a glider through process

herself rotting into process. The corruption in my borough,
entrenched as the bureaucrats who gave the fig to Alighieri,
with a fluke's roll goes under.

I shall not stop with Thucydides, his smashed roof tiles
hurled onto courtyard captives. My threnody is also
for the clay, for their tunnels of air breathing back and forth
on the hinge of midday and mind. A swinging door
pinned under shattered terra-cotta or released to sail
for the clay beds, their sunned seas.

Unfinished Announcement

A deep cough hauls me up and heaves me
into the third night of clear phlegm.

Into the small hours the lamp of the world out.
My bedroom a freighter's crow's nest over barely felt engines.

The changes are coming in, they require
this slowness over dark water.

The maple close by the window needs to extend every nerve
out over an Atlantic sliding like slate beneath it.

In my book still open, a young widower at night has glimpsed
his dead wife in a London blank as a fogged dockyard.

She also stares at him. And slowly they *know*. The whole real deep of it.

She still feels life, life of a kind, carrying her,
muting, absorbing, yet entering the same and leaving the same,

although she knows that change has overtaken her.
The changes need to push through each cell.

The prow needs to hold itself unrustable and gleaming
even down and black, into endless water.

What does a blackbird see, clamped twiggy over the sliding wet slabs?

After the spasms, in lamplight the same yet newly absorbent,
a question newly spreads, I cannot see out of it—

is this strange sameness the great alteration, death's afterward?
Even through the fingers extends difference.

Breathing too differs though it resumes above the slow rushing.
An impulse to leap and bang things, even that dampens.

The test lies in the odd clarity stretching out past finger ends.
Renewal, what everyone has asked for: it extends here.

But this time there are to be no ceremonies.
When morning comes the miracle will go in everywhere.

Dimensions into the photograph, the next red into the painting.
Coming from our houses we shall blink.

Not giving any sign, but full of the knowledge.
For he saw her truly. And seeing him she had been certain.

Coming from our doorways into day, we shall
dispense with any reservations.

Each man, each woman, will carry the opening after shutting it
and be that framelessness. But not dance, not shout.

For only the whole unfolding will let us get the sense of it down,
the entire day, and the night, and the oncoming ocean of night-day.

The swift low swell riding through tamped granulars.
Met eyes vanishing. Unlocking hands filled. Earth, released wave.

Adventus

It came like the traveling circus.
It came in two black carriages and a wagon
to the estate house. Fornication
with cook and servants, soon in the offing,
was only the first hint that all their performance,
before it unfolded in the saloon,
stood miniature. What it came
in order to come to was still coming.

So was coming, and came, and mercifully
widened after drums crinolines repeaters
and grease-paint jammed back into chests,
it broadened out after creaking
leather in the carriages
winnowed itself from hearing and the oblongs
of buttery light in the villa
snuffed themselves. It stayed
in the densifying hill, the arcing poplar windbreak.
And then the screen on which all of this had spread,
the salt-crystal grain of that screen, the spread-out day,
went black and mute. Others got up
and filed out chattering and buttoning coats.
While it, what had come, went on
staying and staying, smell of earth after light rain
and evening siphoning off to far winkings
and the gurgle of a burn,

until the power in me that had been seeing
withered, dropped, while what had come went on staying
until it settled itself
off into the road they had taken
and up into wisping curls from the flue
and tangent in two rakes at an angle
against the stone sill and wet air, settled
as a bed does, or the bogeys beneath an undercarriage, freighting
all of these to a destination
molecularly here yet moving vastly into announcement,
ponderously at grace, graced at porously being ported
as an oar hung
in its oarlock carries into boat, and hand, and river
and the drop at tip-fairing soon to bead and bulge
falling as we say and reenter.

Passage

under the seen, neither lap nor long embrace,
it is like the progress by canal barge out of Dijon
past the lockmasters' houses, and it is like those houses,
each a cottage with geraniums but in squared granite,
fitted out with brass numerals and a hand semaphore
so that through sunny hours the apparition of domestic
singularity and solidity gets stamped with the impress
of Dutch replication, bureaucratic weight, military snap.
But a snap drifting into porosity, dusted with somnolence
of alerts met routinely and the heavy swish of watergates.
On ahead, the arc of an angler's rod under plane trees
just where the flatness, beginning to bend, deceptively
takes its hazed mirrorings and gnat swirls through zero aperture.
It is like the suspension, neither glide nor plunge,
which makes of thick red paint along the ferruled moldings
and tubular handrails a proposition to be decoded
by one of the philosophers of layers, rabbis of Baklava.
There is the truth beyond
                                    question, unquestionably.
Passage, beyond beginning or beginning again,
is its portal, and likeness in passing keeps it open.
Likeness a sunned moth on that handrail: my friend's hand,
and passing is like air in the shore grass after wind,
moisture and scent among the growth on that arm, also
like breath at its cusps, intake or outflow, in the throat's column
unspeaking, hunting no pitch, anticipating no thought.

Motion pressed off bow and sucked off rudder as one swirl.
Like, like: it is like a simile, a comparison stepping off
one stone because it has found another in the amber pour.
Not simply steering down a channel, this voyage. And the thrush begins.

Notes

In my second and third epigraphs I have taken small liberties with the scholarly translations by A. S. B. Glover and Thomas Cleary. Glover's translation appears in the English edition of Marie-Louise von Franz's study of the *Aurora Consurgens*, arguably Thomas Aquinas's last seminar.

The Victorine in "Barn Doorway in July" is Richard of St. Victor. The Seneca prophecy invoked in "Thucydides," which provides me with my title, has been translated and paraphrased in several sources. In "Medley of the Cut," *Signor Mountainous* is Eugenio Montale. In "Letter to Hermann Broch, December 2001," some of the details about displaced children come from Gitta Sereny's memoir of her wartime work with the Auxiliaire Sociale and the UNRRA. In the same poem, George Oppen's phrase *what art is* comes from section 27 in *Of Being Numerous*. The biographer of McNamara in "Transmission Lines" is Paul Hendrickson. "Walter Benjamin's Hope for the Best" borrows Meister Eckhart's phrase about the soul: "Its whole delight is in birth." The following sources support passages in "San Andrean One": Pindar's *Pythian 3*, James Kirsch's *The Reluctant Prophet* (Rabbi Wechsler and Goetz), Susan Griffin's *A Chorus of Stones* (Israel Torres), Victor Weisskopf's *The Joy of Insight: Passions of a Physicist*, and Michael Ortiz Hill's *Dreaming the End of the World* ("Messiah one with the Beast").